What You
Know
Might Not Be
So

What You Know Might Not Be So

220 Misinterpretations of Bible Texts Explained

David C. Downing

BAKER BOOK HOUSE
Grand Rapids, Michigan 49516

Most of the Scripture quotations are from the KJV, King James Version.
There are occasional references to the RSV, Revised Standard Version, ©
1972 by Thomas Nelson, Inc.; NIV, New International Version, © 1978 by
New York International Bible Society; NASB, New American Standard
Bible, © 1960, 1962, 1963, 1968, 1971, 1972, 1973, 1975, 1977 by The Lock-
man Foundation; NEB, New English Bible, © 1961, 1970 by The Delegates of
the Oxford University Press and The Syndics of the Cambridge University
Press; JB, The Jerusalem Bible, © 1966 by Darton, Longman & Todd, Ltd.
and Doubleday & Company, Inc.

Acknowledgments

I make no claim to be an expert on the Bible, but I have received generous assistance and advice from the experts. I wish to thank especially Dr. Robert Bascom, a translation consultant for the United Bible Societies, and his wife, Lois, for their encouragement and support and for their thorough and perceptive reading of the manuscript.

Many thanks also to my colleagues at Westmont College, including Dr. Peter Diamond in Old Testament, Drs. Thomas Schmidt and Robert H. Gundry in New Testament, and Dr. Curtis Whiteman in Church History. Each of these read all or part of the manuscript at various stages, offering some key corrections or suggestions. I am grateful also to Dr. George Blankenbaker, who took an interest in the project both as an Old Testament scholar and as Academic Dean at Westmont. These specialists have helped me greatly in identifying errors and distortions in the manuscript; any errors which remain are, of course, my own responsibility.

Dr. Paul Delaney, Professor of English at Westmont College, and Reed Jolley, a pastor of the Santa Barbara

Community Church, read early drafts of the manuscript and offered many helpful comments.

I am especially indebted to my brother Donald Downing, my principal manuscript editor. Thanks also to my brother Jim Downing for sending me three-hours' worth of engaging, entertaining, and useful remarks on tape about this project. I am grateful as well to my wife, Dr. Crystal Downing; my parents, James and Morena Downing; and my sister, Marobeth Downing Ruegg.

Introduction

Most people are familiar with the Bible, even if they haven't read it for themselves. They know, for example, that Eve ate a forbidden apple, that Jonah was swallowed by a whale, and that Elijah rode to heaven in a fiery chariot. They know that angels have halos and devils have horns.

But what most people know isn't always so. The Bible teaches none of these things. A careful study of Bible conceptions and misconceptions also reveals that words such as *Jehovah* and *Calvary* do not belong in Scripture, why Michelangelo sculpted Moses with horns, and why a Crusader's battle cry should have been a peace slogan. These are just a few of the scores of common misconceptions about the Bible.

Even in today's pluralistic society, the Bible continues to be one of our most widely read and widely quoted books. It is also one of the most frequently *mis*read and *mis*quoted. Sometimes people simply do not read carefully enough. Or they may not understand an ancient expression or custom. Or they don't realize that the English of the KJV (King James Version) is not the English of today. Bible readers may also meaning of Scripture according to their own convictions rather than the other way around.

This handbook explores the most common misconceptions about the Bible. It explains in concise, nontechnical terms the most frequently repeated misunderstandings of Scripture texts. A deliberate effort has been made to avoid doctrinal disputes, sectarian controversies, or perennial questions still open to scholarly debate. Instead these entries focus on matters of simple miscomprehension, contrasting what the Bible actually says to what many people think it says.

It is hoped that this book will not only help correct some oft-heard fallacies about the Bible but also encourage readers to take up the Bible themselves for careful and thoughtful study.

Abbreviations

Books of the Bible

Old Testament

Gn = Genesis
Ex = Exodus
Lv = Leviticus
Nm = Numbers
Dt = Deuteronomy
Jos = Joshua
Jgs = Judges
Ru = Ruth
1 Sm = 1 Samuel
2 Sm = 2 Samuel
1 Kgs = 1 Kings
2 Kgs = 2 Kings
1 Chr = 1 Chronicles
2 Chr = 2 Chronicles
Ezr = Ezra
Neh = Nehemiah
Est = Esther
Jb = Job
Ps(s) = Psalms
Prv = Proverbs

Eccl = Ecclesiastes
Sg = Song
   of Solomon
Is = Isaiah
Jer = Jeremiah
Lam = Lamentations
Ez = Ezekiel
Dn = Daniel
Hos = Hosea
Jl = Joel
Am = Amos
Ob = Obadiah
Jon = Jonah
Mi = Micah
Na = Nahum
Hb = Habukkuk
Zep = Zephaniah
Hag = Haggai
Zec = Zechariah
Mal = Malachi

New Testament

Mt = Matthew
Mk = Mark
Lk = Luke
Jn = John
Acts = Acts of the
  Apostles
Rom = Romans
1 Cor = 1 Corinthians
2 Cor = 2 Corinthians
Gal = Galatians
Eph = Ephesians
Phil = Philippians
Col = Colossians
1 Thes = 1 Thessalonians
2 Thes = 2 Thessalonians

1 Tm = 1 Timothy
2 Tm = 2 Timothy
Ti = Titus
Phlm = Philemon
Heb = Hebrews
Jas = James
1 Pt = 1 Peter
2 Pt = 2 Peter
1 Jn = 1 John
2 Jn = 2 John
3 Jn = 3 John
Jude
Rv = Revelation

English Translations of the Bible

KJV = King James Version
RSV = Revised Standard Version
JB = Jerusalem Bible
NEB = New English Bible
NASB = New American Standard Bible
NIV = New International Version

A

"Abandon all hope ye who enter here"—These famous words are said to be engraved in stone over the gateway to hell. The phrase does not come, however, from Revelation or any other book of the Bible. Rather it is found in Dante's *Inferno*, Canto 3, line 9.

Absalom, hanging by the hair—Even in Bible commentaries, one finds references to Absalom hanging by his hair from the branches of an oak. But the Bible says his head was caught.

Absalom, King David's handsome but rebellious son, died at the battle of Ephraim when his enemies found him dangling from an oak tree and stabbed him to death. The second Book of Samuel explains: "Absalom was riding upon his mule, and the mule went under the thick branches of a great oak, and his head caught fast in the oak, and he was left hanging between heaven and earth, while the mule that was under him went on" (2 Sm 18:9b, RSV).

Some might argue that the word *head* is being used loosely here to signify "head of hair." After all, Absalom was known for his luxuriant hair. It is said he cut it only once a year, shearing off several pounds of hair when it grew heavy on him (2 Sm 14:26). But in other passages the writer of Samuel is careful to distinguish between one's head and the hair on one's head. (See 1 Sm 14:45 and 2 Sm 14:26.)

Adam and Eve, Children of—Many people wrongly suppose that Adam and Eve had only two sons, Cain and Abel. These two sons are most often remembered because of the biblical account of the first murder when Cain killed Abel out of jealousy for the Lord's favor.

If these two were the only offspring of Adam, then it would be left up to Cain, a murderer and an exile, to father the human race. But the Book of Genesis explains that Adam and Eve produced another son, Seth (Gn 4:25).

The Bible does not explain where Cain or Seth found their wives but notes that Adam lived 800 years after the birth of Seth, begetting more sons as well as daughters (Gn 5:4). The exact number is never given.

"Almost persuaded"—There have been countless sermons and more than one hymn about people who are "almost persuaded," who come near to believing but who simply cannot make a final commitment. This familiar theme, however, comes from a phrase in the New Testament which is difficult to translate with any certainty.

The KJV reports that when Paul, in chains, was testifying before King Agrippa and Festus, a Roman official, Agrippa exclaimed, "Almost thou persuadest me to be a Christian" (Acts 26:28). This sounds as if Agrippa himself were on the verge of becoming a convert, but closer examination casts doubt on this interpretation of the phrase.

The Agrippa in this incident is Herod Agrippa II, grandson of the notorious Herod the Great. This Agrippa is known mainly for his attempts, largely unsuccessful, to reconcile Judaism with the Hellenistic world of the Roman Empire. When making his own defense, Paul placed Agrippa in a difficult position by asking him if he believed in the Jewish prophets. If Agrippa answered yes to this question, he would have lost face before his gentile colleague Festus; but by answering no, he was certain to displease the Jews present.

Agrippa changed the subject with an apparently sly remark about how easily Paul thought he could make a new convert. Agrippa's reply to Paul's insistent question translates literally, "In a little, you are persuading me to make a Christian." The unusual verb choice suggests that Agrippa was being evasive and perhaps even sarcastic. The RSV renders this enigmatic phrase: "In a short time, you think to make me a Christian!"

"Ancient of Days"—This phrase occurs three times in the Book of Daniel, where the prophet describes his vision of God as a stately judge with white hair and white robes (7:9–22). The term "ancient of days" has been taken by some readers as a special title for God, a reference to his eternal existence "from everlasting to everlasting."

It should be noted, however, that "ancient of days" is an idiom found in many ancient languages including Aramaic, the language of the section of Daniel in which this phrase occurs. The general sense of the term is simply "very old." This may connote a wise and

13

venerable age, but it does not, in itself, suggest super-human longevity. So the author of Daniel is not using a special name for God in this passage; rather he is adapting a familiar idiom for his own descriptive purposes.

Angels with halos—Contrary to the way they are nearly always pictured, angels in the Bible are never described as having halos.

In both Hebrew and Greek, the word usually translated "angel" means simply "messenger." The biblical accounts do not emphasize how angels look or what sort of beings they are, but rather their roles as messengers, harbingers, guardians, or instruments of punishment.

Except for the seraphim and cherubim, angels in the Bible are pictured as having human form. Generally they are not identified by any distinguishing physical features but rather by their unusual powers and by the messages they convey from God. Several times in the Bible angelic visitors are not even recognized at first as anything other than humans (Gn 19:1–15; Jgs 6:11–22; Acts 1:10–11).

Of course, angels don't always travel incognito. In New Testament accounts especially, angels who appear to humans often possess a dazzling radiance. This brilliant luminosity seems to be what strikes fear into the hearts of those who see them. When an angel appears to the shepherds announcing Christ's birth, Luke writes, "The glory of the Lord shone round about them" (2:9). And when an angel announces Christ's resurrection to the women who came to Jesus' tomb, he has a "countenance like lightning" (Mt 28:2–3).

Note, though, how little these descriptions resemble the usual picture of a halo, a soft, sacred aura behind the head. Medieval and renaissance painters frequently used halos to adorn the heads of angels, as they did in depictions of Jesus, his parents, and numerous saints. Halos are said symbolically to represent a person as hallowed (hence the word *halo*), but they are not meant to convey anything about the actual appearance of saints or angels.

Angels with harps—In the popular imagination, angels spend most of their time reclining on clouds strumming their harps. But angels are never portrayed with harps in the Bible.

Angels are depicted in Scripture blessing God and praising his name, but nowhere are they described using harps to accompany their hymns. The Psalms frequently refer to humans using harps in their praise of God but not to angels with harps. Actually, the stringed instrument referred to in many psalms is better translated "lyre."

Apple, as the Forbidden Fruit—From medieval paintings to modern billboards, Eve is nearly always portrayed reaching for an all-too-tempting apple. But the forbidden fruit in the biblical account of the Fall is never identified as an apple or any other kind of actual fruit.

The Book of Genesis says that God placed in the Garden of Eden "every tree that is pleasant to the sight, and good for food; the tree of life also in the midst of the garden, and the tree of knowledge of good and evil" (2:9). This suggests that the Garden of Eden contained every regular kind of fruit tree plus the tree of life and

15

Madonna and Child with Angels and Cherubim; Matteo di Giovanni; National Gallery of Art, Washington; Andrew W. Mellon Collection.

The Fall of Man; Albrecht Alt-dorfer, workshop of; National Gallery of Art, Washington; Samuel H. Kress Collection.

the tree of the knowledge of good and evil. Nowhere are these last two trees identified with any kind of tree known today, apple or otherwise.

Tom Burnam, in *The Dictionary of Misinformation*, speculates that the forbidden fruit might better be pictured as an apricot rather than an apple, given the climate of the region where the Garden of Eden was said to be located. But such conjecture seems fruitless since the tree of knowledge is clearly differentiated from the more common trees. There has been only one tree of the knowledge of good and evil—and its fruit has been out of season since the Fall.

"Apple of the eye"—This charming phrase is generally thought of as a biblical idiom, and indeed it appears five times in the Old Testament. Literally, it refers to the pupil of the eye, but it is commonly used in a figurative sense, connoting something that one holds precious and keeps a watchful eye on. Thus David can pray to the Lord: "Keep me as the apple of the eye, hide me under the shadow of thy wings" (Ps 17:8).

17

Though the phrase has a certain biblical flavor to it, it is not found in the original Hebrew. Rather, it is a traditional English idiom going all the way back to the time of the Anglo-Saxons. English translators borrowed the metaphor because the comparable Hebrew idiom wouldn't make much sense to English readers. The Hebrews referred to the pupil as the "little man of the eye," perhaps referring to the reflected image one may see in another's eyes.

Ararat, as the resting place of Noah's ark—In this century there have been a half dozen major expeditions to the eastern border of Turkey in search of Noah's ark. Following clues in the eighth chapter of Genesis, explorers have hoped to find remains of the craft preserved in the glacial ice to prove that the voyage of Noah is not just an ancient story but ancient history. Though these expeditions have centered on a mountain thought to be the Mount Ararat of biblical times, the Genesis account does not make it abundantly clear on which peak the ark came to rest.

Genesis 8:4 refers to the ark coming to rest "upon the mountains of Ararat," a whole range of mountains, not one specific peak. The mountains of Ararat, the Armenian highlands in modern Turkey, cover hundreds of square miles, and there is more than one tradition about which mountain is *the* mountain where Noah's ark came to rest. European tradition favors the twin peaks called Massis by the Armenians, also named Big Ararat and Little Ararat. The taller of these peaks with an elevation over 17,200 feet is the highest peak in the region. Islamic tradition, though, identifies Noah's mountain with Jebel Judi, considerably farther south.

One ancient authority, Berosus the Chaldean, places the mount of Noah as far away as Kurdistan.

Ark of the covenant as a weapon—Contrary to its depiction in the popular media, the biblical ark of the covenant was not a battle weapon. It was a portable shrine that assured the Israelites that the Lord went before them in the wilderness and in war.

The ark was a wooden chest overlaid with gold inside and out and topped by a solid gold lid. The lid, called the mercy seat, was hammered into the form of two cherubs facing each other with outspread wings (Ex 25:10–22). Since the Hebrews pictured God enthroned above the cherubim (Ps 18:10; Ez 10:1), they saw the ark not just as a sacred container, but as a portable throne for God. When the ark was carried before the people of Israel, they envisioned the Lord himself going before them. (*See also* MERCY SEAT and CHERUBS.)

The ark of the covenant was so named because it represented the covenant that the Lord made with the Hebrew people during the time of Moses. Inside the chest were stone tablets with the Ten Commandments on them; the rod of Moses' brother Aaron, which had miraculously bloomed; and a bowl of manna, the "bread from heaven," which God provided for his people in the wilderness. All of these were reminders of God's special care for his people.

The Israelites did indeed carry the ark before them in their battles to take possession of Canaan, the promised land. The ark was not considered a weapon to use against Israel's enemies; rather, it assured the Hebrews of the Lord's continuing presence with them and the continuing exercise of his power in their behalf.

The ark did possess awesome and mysterious powers, according to biblical accounts. It was to be transported only by priests with special carrying-poles to prevent anyone from touching it. Once when the ark was being carried in a cart instead of on carrying-poles, an Israelite reached out to steady the ark when the oxen pulling the cart stumbled. When he touched it, he fell dead on the spot (2 Sm 6:2–7). Another time at least seventy men were slain for looking into the ark (1 Sm 6:19, RSV). When the Philistines captured the ark, they were afflicted by tumors and mice until they returned it to the people of Israel (1 Sm 4–6). These incidents do not portray the ark of the covenant as a battle weapon; rather, they underscore its sacred character and its unique connection with the Israelites.

Arks in the Old Testament—The English word *ark*, a wooden chest or container, is used in the KJV to stand for two different Hebrew words in the Old Testament. This has led to some confusion between Noah's ark and the ark of the covenant.

In the story of Noah the ark was, of course, a kind of boat, the giant craft he built to escape the flood (Gn 6–8). Moses, too, floated to safety in an ark—an "ark of bulrushes" made by his mother to protect her newborn son from a pharaoh's cruel edict (Ex 2:1–6).

The ark of the covenant, though sometimes pictured in illustrations as a miniature boat, was a portable chest made to be carried on poles, not to float. The Hebrew word for this ark is totally unrelated to the term used to designate the ark of Noah.

"Ashes to ashes, dust to dust"—This phrase is not found in Scripture. It comes from the Anglican *Book of Common Prayer.*

The phrase echoes biblical passages about death and mourning with their assertion that the body without the spirit is no more than dust and ashes (Gn 3:19; 18:27; Jb 30:19). But the actual wording "ashes to ashes, dust to dust" comes from the *Book of Common Prayer*'s service for burial of the dead:

> Unto Almighty God we commend the soul of our *brother* departed, and we commit *his* body to the ground; earth to earth, ashes to ashes, dust to dust: in sure and certain hope of the resurrection unto eternal life, through our Lord Jesus Christ.

"At ease in Zion"—The phrase "at ease in Zion" is occasionally quoted as if it refers to a time of peace and plenty for God's people in Jerusalem. But the phrase comes from a prophet's warning against false security and his prediction of impending judgment.

Amos, chapter 6, begins "Woe to them that are at ease in Zion." It goes on to describe the people of Jerusalem living in leisure and luxury unaware that their destruction is near. "At ease in Zion" in this context does not refer to the comfort of those near to God, but to the complacency of those who are far from him.

21

B

Balm in Gilead—With violence in the Middle East an almost daily occurrence, school children have increasingly been heard asking their parents or teachers about that ominous bomb in Gilead.

Of course, the correct term is the "balm in Gilead." This is best known from the traditional spiritual which proclaims the efficacy of the balm:

> There is a balm in Gilead to make the wounded whole;
> There is a balm in Gilead to heal the sin-sick soul.

In the Old Testament, though, the emphasis is just the opposite: the balm is *unable* to cure the spiritual ills of God's people. The prophet Jeremiah attributes the sickness of the nation Israel to its abandonment of God, a sickness beyond earthly remedies: "Is there no balm in Gilead; is there no physician there? Why then is not the health of the daughter of my people recovered?" (Jer 8:22).

Gilead, a tableland east of the Jordan River, was known in ancient times for its medicinal balm, an important item of local commerce. It was probably made from a fragrant resin, though no one knows from which plant. Scholars agree, though, that the lotion peddled to modern-day tourists in Israel has little claim to be the same as the genuine "balm in Gilead."

"Barbarous people"—Luke's reference to the "barbarous people" of Malta does not suggest savagery on their part nor bigotry on his part.

After Paul and his companions, Luke among them, were shipwrecked on their way to Rome, they came safely to shore on the island of Malta ("Melita" in the KJV). There, according to Luke, the "barbarous people" who lived on the island showed "no little kindness" to the castaways (Acts 28:2).

The word used to describe the islanders, both in New Testament Greek and in King James English, does not imply that these were uncouth or uncivilized people. Rather it means "foreigners, non-Greeks." The word is apparently an echo of what unknown languages sounded like to those who spoke Greek: "bar bar bar bar. . . ."

Since the word *barbarous* now carries strong connotations of cruelty or savagery, twentieth-century translations of this passage employ neutral words like *inhabitants* or *natives* to describe these compassionate and "unbarbarous" islanders.

B.C. and A.D.—The abbreviations B.C. and A.D. do not originate anywhere in Scripture. A.D. appeared in the sixth century, and B.C. did not come into common usage until the seventeenth century.

A.D. is short for Latin *anno domini,* "in the year of [our] Lord." The abbreviation first appeared about A.D. 525, an innovation of monastic scribes who did not

23

think that church history should be reckoned according to a secular event, the founding of Rome.

A.D. is sometimes taken to stand for "After Death" (of Christ). But, of course, that explanation will not work since it does not explain why events during Christ's own lifetime are dated A.D. If years were numbered starting with Christ's death rather than his birth, we would have to subtract about thirty-three years from every date in the last two millenia. (*See* BIRTHDATE OF CHRIST.)

B.C. means simply "before Christ" and is not a translation of any Latin phrase. For centuries after the invention of A.D., historians still dated events before Christ's birth according to a calendar based on the founding of Rome. Eventually someone realized that one could count backward as well as forward from the birth of Christ, and the abbreviation B.C. replaced earlier methods of reckoning the years.

Bearing one another's burdens—Some readers who look for such things suppose they have found a contradiction in the sixth chapter of Galatians. In verse 2, Paul exhorts his readers to "bear ye one another's burdens, and so fulfill the law of Christ." In verse 5 Paul seems to give the exact opposite advice: "For every man shall bear his own burden." This seeming contradiction arises from translating two different Greek words with the same English word *burden*.

When speaking of bearing one another's burdens in verse 2, Paul uses the plural of the Greek word *baryos*, "a heavy or burdensome weight." The same root gives us the modern English words *barium*, originally found in a heavy ore, and *barometer*, an instrument to measure the "heaviness" of the air (air pressure). When

24

baryos is used in the New Testament, it nearly always carries explicit connotations of something burdensome. (*See* Mt 20:12, Lk 11:46, or Acts 15:28.) In fact, some modern translations replace the word *burdens* in this verse with "heavy loads" (NEB) or "troubles" (JB).

The Greek word in verse 5 translated also as burden in the KJV is *phortion*, "something carried." The same word is used in Matthew 11:30, where Jesus says, "For my yoke is easy and my burden is light." The base of *phortion* appears, in rather disguised form, in the modern English words "trans*port*ation and *port*able. This word does not have the same connotations of a wearisome load that *baryos* does.

Verses 2 and 5 in the sixth chapter of Galatians should not be seen as contradictory but complementary. Paul suggests that each person should carry his or her own load but also help others who are overburdened with the loads they have to carry.

Commentators point out as well that Paul instructs Christians to bear one another's burdens (present tense), adding that each shall be (future tense) responsible for his or her own load. This suggests that we try to lighten each other's burdens now but that all must answer to God on the day of reckoning for their own conduct.

"Be still and know that I am God"—This statement from Psalm 46:10 is almost always treated as a command to quiet one's soul—to put aside all the day's haste and hustle and to contemplate serenely the majesty and sovereignty of God. Though this kind of meditation is recommended elsewhere in Scripture, that is not the meaning of this phrase.

"Be still" is not an invitation to draw apart from the conflicts and anxieties of life; it is a literal command to cease fighting. The passage in which the phrase appears concerns God's sovereignty over Israel and over her enemies:

> He makes wars cease to the end of the earth; he breaks the bow, and shatters the spear, he burns the chariots with fire! Be still and know that I am God. I am exalted among the nations, I am exalted in the earth (Ps 46:9–10, RSV).

Beulah Land—Occasionally one will hear a radio preacher talk about "going to Beulah Land" as if the term is synonymous with heaven. It is not a name for heaven, but for the restored nation of Israel.

Beulah Land is probably best known from the traditional hymn with this chorus:

> O Beulah Land, sweet Beulah Land
> As on thy highest mount I stand,
> I look away across the sea,
> Where mansions are prepared for me,
> And view the shining glory-shore,
> My heaven, my home forevermore.

If church-goers drowse during the hymn, they would only catch the first and last lines of this chorus and assume that Beulah is a synonym for heaven. But notice that the hymn-writer envisions himself standing on the highest mount in Beulah Land while gazing over to heaven.

The Hebrew word *Beulah*, which means "married," is used in the Book of Isaiah as an allegorical name for

26

the restored nation of Israel. The prophet foresees a glorious future day when the land will no longer be called "Desolate," but "Married" (Is 62:4–5).

Birthdate of Jesus—The actual day and year of Christ's birth can only be conjectured. Neither the day, December 25, nor the year, A.D. 1, is based on the evidence of the New Testament nativity accounts.

The day of Christ's birth is not specified in the Gospel accounts. Luke says that there were shepherds tending their flocks by night (2:8), an action which would seem unlikely in December, the beginning of the rainy season in Palestine. Various birthdates for Jesus were put forward in the early church including January 6, March 25, April 19, August 28, and November 17. Not one of these was convincingly demonstrated, however, or accepted by the church at large.

It was not until A.D. 354 that December 25 was officially designated as the day to celebrate Christ's birth. Not all of Christendom accepted this date, proclaimed by Bishop Lucius of Rome. (December 25 may have been chosen because it coincided with a Roman festival of the winter solstice.) Even now the Eastern Orthodox Church celebrates Christmas thirteen days later.

Our present calendar is based on the assumption that Jesus was born at the beginning of A.D. 1, but that date does not harmonize with the chronology of the Gospels. Matthew says that Christ was born during the reign of King Herod, who died in 4 B.C. Scholars date the birth of Christ between 7 B.C. and 4 B.C., depending on how they interpret the information in Matthew, chapter 2. Verses 13–15 say that Joseph took Jesus to live in Egypt until Herod's death, and verse 16 says that Herod commanded all the children in Bethlehem aged two or less to be slaughtered. It can only be guessed whether this barbarous edict came a full two years after Christ's birth or if Herod was allowing himself a margin of safety.

Blaspheming the Holy Spirit—The English poet William Cowper (1731–1800) suffered for many years under the morbid fear that he had committed the unpardonable sin. Though he provided the words for a half dozen hymns still sung today, Cowper was oppressed by a sense that he had offended God beyond forgiveness by "blaspheming the Holy Spirit." His very fear about committing the unpardonable sin should have reassured him that he had not done so.

The doctrine of the unpardonable sin comes from Jesus' warning about blaspheming the Holy Spirit. When the Pharisees saw Jesus performing miraculous healings and casting out demons, they did not deny his wonder-working power. Rather, they claimed that his power came from Beelzebub, "the prince of demons" (Mt 12:22–24). Jesus answered that a house divided against itself cannot stand and that Satan cannot work against Satan. Jesus continued with this ominous warning:

> Therefore I tell you, every sin and blasphemy shall be forgiven men, but the blasphemy against the Spirit will not be forgiven. And whoever says a word against the Son of man will be forgiven; but whoever speaks against the Holy Spirit will not be forgiven, either in this age or in the age to come (Mt 12:31–32, RSV).

There is still some lively discussion about the exact meaning of this teaching, but interpreters agree on two things. First, the context of Jesus' words is crucial to an understanding of them. Jesus had been performing great works by divine power, but the Pharisees chose to label his powers satanic rather than to reconsider their own convictions. It is this kind of obstinate unbelief which can render one's soul irredeemably lost. Second, it should be remembered that, according to the Bible, the Holy Spirit is the one who brings conviction of sin and a desire for repentance (Jn 16:7–11). To reject this work of the Spirit persistently and deliberately is to place oneself beyond the pale of God's redemption.

Jesus' warning about blaspheming the Holy Spirit, taken in the larger context of all his teachings, refers not to some impulsive, unforgivable profanity directed at the Holy Spirit; rather it refers to the adamant resistance of one's heart to the testimony and convicting power of the Spirit. William Cowper, and others who fret about the unpardonable sin, may take comfort that their very anxiety proves they have not reached this state of spiritual imperviousness.

"Bosom of Abraham"—"Rock-a my soul in the bosom of Abraham" say the words of the well-known spiritual. And those who sing the song usually picture themselves, or their souls, nestled warm and protected in the lap of Father Abraham. But the Hebrew idiom used by Jesus in Luke 16 has somewhat different connotations.

In Luke 16:19–31, Jesus tells the parable of the rich man and Lazarus. The rich man "was clothed in purple and fine linen and fared sumptuously every day," while the beggar Lazarus lay outside his gate, covered with sores and begging for the crumbs which fell from the

29

rich man's table. But when the two died, Lazarus was "carried by the angels into Abraham's bosom" (v. 22), while the rich man went to Hades, pictured in this parable as a place of thirst and torment.

To his Jewish listeners, Jesus' reference to "Abraham's bosom" would call forth the image of a great banquet with Abraham as the host and Lazarus as the guest of honor. On feast days and other special occasions, the custom among the Jews in Jesus' day was to dine at a low U-shaped table as they reclined on pillows. The guest of honor reclined at the right hand of the host with his head almost on his chest, or bosom. This is what John's Gospel refers to when it speaks of one of the disciples, probably John himself, "leaning on Jesus' bosom" at the Last Supper (Jn 13:23).

While Lazarus suffered hunger and deprivation during his life, he joined the great feast of the righteous dead, headed by the father of his race, after his life was over. Jesus paints a similar picture in Matthew 8:11, when he says that "Many shall come from east and west [i.e., non-Jews], and shall sit with Abraham, Isaac, and Jacob, in the kingdom of heaven."

Burying one's father—When Jesus called on his listeners to follow him, one of them answered with a request: "Lord, suffer me first to go and bury my father." Jesus answered, "Follow me; and let the dead bury their dead" (Mt 8:21–22).

Jesus' response to the would-be disciple seems unduly harsh on first reading. After all, shouldn't a faithful son be allowed a time of mourning? Perhaps the proper funeral arrangements have yet to be made. Or perhaps his bereaved family needs the strength and support of a son and brother.

But in all likelihood the man's father was not actually dead. The Hebrew expression "let me bury my
father" does not mean "my father has just died."
Rather, it was used to put off someone's request into
the indefinite future with a vague reference to other
obligations. The general sense of the expression is
"until my father grows old and dies, I can't act on your
request." Travelers in the Middle East today report
that this idiom is still used there as a form of polite
refusal.

C

Caduceus from the brazen serpent—Some readers of the Bible have assumed incorrectly that the caduceus, the symbol of the medical profession, is derived from the healing serpent of Moses. However, the caduceus comes to us from the Greeks, not the Hebrews.

The caduceus usually takes the form of a winged staff with one or two serpents entwined around it. This staff is associated with Asclepius, the Greek god of healing (and also with Hermes, the messenger of the gods.) The story behind this unusual symbol is lost in prehistory, though snakes are associated in many ancient cultures with the power to curse and to cure.

This dual power is especially evident in the biblical account of Moses and the brass serpent (Nm 21:4–9). When the Israelites wandered in the desert after escaping from Egypt, more than once they spoke out against God and against Moses. On one occasion when they complained about the insufficient food and water, they were beset by "fiery serpents" (interpreted as "poisonous snakes" in some modern translations). Many who were bitten died. When the Israelites repented, the

Lord instructed Moses to fashion a brass serpent and to place it on a pole. ("Brass" is in the KJV; all modern translations correct this to "bronze.") When those who were bitten looked at this serpent, they were healed.

Though this incident is not the origin of the caduceus insignia, it is the source of one of the most striking allusions in the New Testament. Referring to his coming crucifixion, Jesus said, "And as Moses lifted up the serpent in the wilderness, even so must the Son of man be lifted up; that whosoever believeth in him should not perish but have eternal life" (Jn 3:14–15).

Cain, Mark of—The mark of Cain was not a brand placed on him by the Lord identifying him for life as his brother's murderer. The mark was not an indication of the Lord's curse. Quite the opposite. After killing his brother Abel, Cain pleaded with the Lord, claiming that if he wandered the earth as a fugitive he would have no one to protect him and he himself would be slain. The Lord then set a mark upon Cain as a sign of protection, not as a curse (Gn 4:10–15).

Notice that Cain did not fear he would be killed because he was a murderer. He feared for his life because he would be traveling in exile without family and without a kinsman to act as blood-avenger. In primitive societies where there was no centralized authority, a key deterrent to violent crime was the fear of reprisal from the victim's kinsmen.

Calvary—The site of Jesus' crucifixion is not called Calvary in the texts of the Gospels. And despite the many references in hymns to the "hill of Calvary" or even "Mount Calvary," there is no biblical or archaeological evidence to support the popular idea that the place of execution was on a hill.

The setting of the crucifixion is identified in all four Gospels as a place outside the city called "The Skull" (Mt 27:33, Mk 15:22, Lk 23:33, Jn 19:17). Matthew, Mark, and John identify the site by its Aramaic name, Golgotha, giving also the Greek translation, *kranion*. (This is the root of the medical name for the skull, *cranium*.)

Luke also calls the execution site "The Skull" (Greek *kranion*), which appears in the Latin Vulgate Bible as "the place of the skull" *(calvariae locus)*. When the Latin Bible was translated into English (Rheims, 1582), the Latin wording was retained as a proper name, "Calvary." The KJV retained the Rheims translation, but all modern English versions use the English "skull."

Modern visitors to Jerusalem are shown a hill outside the old city which is said to be the site of the crucifixion. With enough imagination, one can even see a skull-like form in the side of the bluff with two shallow caves forming eye sockets. But Golgotha is never identified in the Bible as a hill, nor is there any archaeological evidence to support that popular belief.

Candle, candlestick—References to candles and candlesticks in the KJV are anachronistic. The candles we use today, wicks encased in wax or tallow, are not mentioned in the Bible. Modern English translations use "lamp" and "lampstand" where the KJV says "candle" and "candlestick."

Catholic Epistles—The "Catholic Epistles" are not

epistles with special reference to or relevance to Catholics, as apart from Protestants.

The word *catholic* comes from a Latin root meaning "universal, general." The Catholic Epistles were so designated by the early church because they were seen as being addressed to church members in general, not the members of any particular congregation. The epistles of Paul were originally written to specific churches to address local circumstances, and they are known by the names of the congregations to whom they were initially sent (e.g., Galatians, Ephesians, Colossians). The Catholic Epistles, on the other hand, are known by the names of those traditionally thought to be their authors: James, Peter, Jude, and John.

The title *Catholic Church* means literally "The Church Universal." That is the reason we find even in Protestant creeds the affirmation, "I believe in the holy catholic and apostolic church." The "Roman Catholic Church" is a paradoxical title, since the very existence of Protestant denominations renders the Roman Church something less than universal. The designation *Protestant* isn't any more precise, since Protestant congregations have defined themselves for centuries by what they affirm, not by what they protest against.

Chains of pride—Bible teachers warning about the dangers of pride occasionally quote from the Book of Psalms: "Therefore pride compasseth them about as a chain" (Ps 73:6). This phrase from the KJV is taken to mean that the proud are bound and shackled by their own conceit without even knowing it.

But the chain mentioned in Psalm 73 is not one of bondage but one of adornment—a necklace. The same word is used in Proverbs 1:8, 9: "My son, hear the in-

35

struction of thy father, and forsake not the law of thy mother: for they shall be an ornament of grace unto thy head, and chains about thy neck."

Chapter and verse—One of the foundational principles of Bible interpretation is that verses must be considered in context. In matters of biblical exegesis, position is nine-tenths of the law. Yet verses are commonly torn out of context, ripped and bleeding, and interpreted as if each were a detachable unit of meaning. This tendency might be lessened if readers knew that chapter and verse divisions were not added until more than a thousand years after the last of the Bible manuscripts was written.

The earliest Bible manuscripts would have been difficult to read, even for one who knew the original languages. Ancient Hebrew writing had no vowels, so the Old Testament text was established by Jewish textual scholars called the Masoretes in the early Middle Ages. The oldest Greek manuscripts of the New Testament do not include the spaces between words, so scholars have had to decide word divisions long before they considered chapter and verse divisions.

In the early decades of the thirteenth century, Stephen Langton, later the Archbishop of Canterbury, divided the Latin Vulgate Bible into chapters. The Old Testament was first divided into verses in 1448 and the New Testament in 1551. The first Bible with chapter and verse divisions was the Geneva Bible, published in 1560, more than 1400 years after the last of the Bible manuscripts was written.

"Chariots of fire"—When the popular film *Chariots of Fire* was released in 1981, newspaper letters-to-the-editor columns were much taken up with the origin of the film's title. Some writers referred to the fiery chariot of Elijah as the source, while others pointed to more obscure references in the Old Testament. The title does not come directly from Scripture at all, but from the English hymn being sung in an early scene of the movie. (*See also* FIERY CHARIOT.)

The film story begins with the funeral of Harold Abrahams, one of the two British runners awarded gold medals in the 1924 Olympics. The congregation is shown singing a hymn universally recognized in England but not so well known in America. The words come from a poem by William Blake:

> And did those feet in ancient time
> Walk upon England's mountains green?
> And was the holy Lamb of God
> On England's pleasant pastures seen?
>
> And did the Countenance Divine
> Shine forth upon our clouded hills?
> And was Jerusalem builded here
> Among these dark Satanic Mills?
>
> Bring me my Bow of burning gold:
> Bring me my arrows of desire:
> Bring me my spear: O clouds unfold!
> Bring me my Chariot of fire.
>
> I will not cease from mental fight,
> Nor shall my Sword sleep in my hand
> Till we have built Jerusalem
> In England's green and pleasant Land.

The central idea in this mystical hymn seems to be that the transcendent realities revealed in the Bible can, through imagination and discipline, be present also in England. That is an appropriate note to sound in a film about a Christian athlete whose physical fortitude is linked to his faith and a Jewish athlete whose strength of will comes from a passion to be the unbeaten standard bearer of his people.

Charity—In today's English the word *charity* is largely associated with donations to the needy or to institutions which serve the needy. In King James English charity did not refer to almsgiving. It was used to translate the Greek word *agape,* defined as the kind of self-giving love which is best revealed in the nature of God himself.

Thus in Paul's famous exposition in 1 Corinthians 13, the word *charity* in the KJV refers to the highest of human loves and the clearest reflection of God:

> And though I bestow all my goods to feed the poor, and though I give my body to be burned, and have not charity, it profiteth me nothing. Charity suffereth long, and is kind; charity envieth not; charity vaunteth not itself, is not puffed up. . . . And now abideth faith, hope, charity, these three; but the greatest of these is charity (1 Cor 13:3–4, 13).

Cherubs—The proud parents who call their baby "a little cherub" are unwittingly describing their infant as a powerful winged creature with four faces and a body like polished bronze.

In the Bible cherubs (or "cherubim," the Hebrew plural) are not cherry-cheeked infants floating innocently in azure skies. They are formidable celestial

The winged child-angel familiar in Renaissance art is more properly called a *putto* or cupid. *Putto with Arms of Jacques Coene;* National Gallery of Art, Washington; Samuel H. Kress Collection.

The cherubim referred to in the Bible are formidable guardians of holy places, similar to this winged ox standing at the gate of an ancient Assyrian palace. *Ashurnasirpal II;* The British Museum.

beings who guard sacred places and on whose backs the Lord himself is said to ride (Ps 18:10).

Biblical descriptions of the cherubim are highly figurative and not always easy to visualize. The most detailed picture occurs in the Book of Ezekiel, where the prophet sees the Lord enthroned above four celestial creatures, each with four wings and four faces. (All the "fours" symbolize their ability to watch and to move in all directions.) Each cherub has a face of a man, of a lion, of an ox, and of an eagle. These four faces proba-

39

bly signify its intelligence, ferocity, strength, and mobility, respectively (Ez 1:5–14).

As illustrated by Ezekiel's vision, cherubim are generally associated with the holy presence of the Lord. After Adam and Eve's disobedience, cherubim are sent to guard the tree of life from humans (Gn 3:24). Later, the figures of two cherubim are placed atop the ark of the covenant, signifying the Lord's enthronement and guarding the sacred articles inside (Ex 25:17–20). Finally, in the apostle John's vision of the apocalypse, creatures like the cherubim appear once more, again as watchful guardians above whom God is enthroned.

The evolution of cherubs in the popular mind from powerful guardians to darling infant-angels is a gradual and curious one. Though the Bible offers no precise angelology, it was believed in the Middle Ages that there were nine orders of angels. The seraphim were the highest order, representing love. Then came the cherubim, whose special attribute was knowledge or contemplation of God. Thus, the eminent medieval theologian Thomas Aquinas was called the "Cherubic Doctor," not because he had a ruddy baby-face, but because he had an incisive theological mind.

By Shakespeare's time a cherub (spelled cherubin) came to be associated with a beautiful or "angelic" woman. Thus, when Othello suspects his wife of unfaithfulness, he sarcastically calls her a "young and rose-lipped cherubin" (II.2.62). Not until the eighteenth century did the word *cherub* take on its modern sense as reference to an innocent child. The cherubim of the Bible then are not to be visualized as floating babes but as awesome celestial beings.

Christ as a name—The term *Jesus Christ* is sometimes

referred to as if it were a first name and last name. But surnames, in the modern sense, were not in use among the common people in Jesus' time. He would have been known simply as Jesus, Joseph's son, or Jesus of Nazareth. The term *Christ* is a title given to Jesus; it is a Greek translation of Messiah, "the Anointed One."

Christian—Since the New Testament centers on the life of Christ and the founding of the Christian church, one would expect the term *Christian* to appear regularly in the text. But the word appears only three times in the New Testament, each time as a reference to what others call the followers of Jesus, not what they call themselves.

Early followers of Jesus designated themselves by many names. In the Book of Acts alone they are called "believers" (5:12), "the disciples" (6:1), "the Way" (9:2), "the saints" (9:13), and "the brethren" (9:30). But they do not refer to themselves as Christians.

Acts 11:26 reports that believers were first called Christians in Antioch, a gentile city. King Agrippa uses the word in referring to the apostle Paul's persuasive powers (Acts 26:28). And 1 Peter 4:16 advises that a man should not be ashamed if he suffers "as a Christian," suggesting the term a persecutor would use in identifying a believer.

Though the term *Christian* simply means "follower of Christ," many scholars believe that it originally had condescending or contemptuous connotations—as did *Protestant, Puritan, Quaker, Methodist, Mennonite,* and the popular names of many other religious groups.

Christmas—Many of the traditions we associate with Christmas—December 25, the decorated tree, the yule

41

log, holly, and mistletoe—do not originate in the Bible or in the early church.

Christmas, the Mass of Christ, was not among the earliest festivals of the church. In fact, one of the most influential church fathers, Origen, objected to the celebration of Jesus' nativity, saying that Christ should not be honored as if he were an earthly ruler. Not until the middle of the fourth century was December 25 settled on, and even that date was not accepted throughout Christendom. (*See also* BIRTHDATE OF JESUS.)

For centuries the Mass of Christ was strictly a religious observance. But as the Germanic nations became evangelized, their traditions and customs began to blend in to make Christmas both a holy day and a holiday. Our Christmas customs involving trees and greenery originate in pagan festivals of the winter solstice. The Germans decorated the Tannenbaum, the Druids gathered mistletoe, and the Saxons wore holly and ivy—all plants that stay green in winter. The Nordic yule season (akin to our word *jolly*) was a time to drink hot wassail and to build bonfires to encourage the winter sun.

The Puritans refused to celebrate Christmas, even as a day of rest, because they considered it an excuse for pagan festivities. Those who protest that Christmas nowadays has lost the spirit of Christ may be surprised to learn just how many traditional yuletide customs do not come from the Bible or from Christianity.

"Circle of the earth"—In comparing God's greatness to man's weakness, the Book of Isaiah declares, "It is he that sitteth upon the circle of the earth, and the inhabitants thereof are as grasshoppers" (Is 40:22a). This reference to the earth as a circle has been taken by some commentators as evidence that the ancient Hebrews were far ahead of their time, conceiving of the earth as a globe. C. I. Scofield, for example, cites this verse as "a remarkable reference to the sphericity of the earth."

But the word Hebrew word *circle* in this context refers to the circle of the horizon or to the vault of sky over one's head. In fact, the same word is rendered "vault" in the NASB. It appears in the NIV's translation of Proverbs 8:27 as "horizon."

The peoples of the ancient Middle East generally conceived of the earth as a flat disc covered by a solid dome, which was held up at the edges of the horizon by mountain pillars or by the sea. One may argue that the Hebrews, because of the divine revelation given to them, did not share this conception, but evidence for that assertion must be found elsewhere. The word *circle* in Isaiah 40:22 cannot be taken as a clear reference to a sphere.

Cities of refuge—The cities of refuge mentioned in the Old Testament were not places where murderers could retreat to escape punishment; rather, they were places where the accidental manslayer could claim asylum until his case was heard before a gathering of impartial judges.

The Israelites established six cities of refuge in Canaan where manslayers could claim asylum and take refuge from any potential avengers of their victims (Nm 35:9–15). These cities of refuge were only for those who had unintentionally taken a life. They gave the person who had committed involuntary manslaughter a chance for a fair hearing before he was tracked down by vengeful kinsmen of the victim.

43

"Cleanliness is next to godliness"—This well-known proverb is not found in the Bible. It comes from a sermon by John Wesley, the eighteenth-century English evangelist who co-founded the Methodist movement with his brother Charles. In his printed version of the sermon, Wesley placed the proverb in quotation marks, suggesting that he did not originate the saying but simply popularized it.

Coat of many colors, Joseph's—Joseph's famous garment wasn't a "coat of many colors." And his brothers' jealousy of him was probably something more than petty covetousness.

Joseph was his father Jacob's favorite, both "the son of his old age" (Gn 37:3) and the son of his most beloved wife, Rachel. Joseph's brothers were the sons of Jacob and Leah, Rachel's sister, whom Jacob was tricked into marrying by her father.

Jacob made a special garment for Joseph, which is called a "coat of many colors" in the KJV. The Hebrew phrase occurs nowhere else in the Bible, so its exact meaning can only be conjectured. But the uncertainty of the KJV translators is evident in the text. The word *many* does not appear in the original Hebrew, so it is placed in italics. Note also that the word *colors* is given an alternative rendering in the margin, *pieces*. Confronted with the puzzling phrase, "a coat with pieces," the translators apparently decided that the pieces were of different colors and, therefore, labeled it an especially brilliant garment. Such a translation makes the brothers' wrath against Joseph seem rather trivial, similar to children quarreling about who got the best Christmas present.

44

Modern translations generally refer to Jacob's gift to Joseph as a "long robe with sleeves." Among today's Bedouin tribes, this type of long-sleeved tunic is worn only by the head of a tribe and by the man chosen to be his heir. In all likelihood, Joseph's older brothers were not incensed by the coat because it was more resplendent than anything in their wardrobe. To them it represented Jacob's intention to pass over the sons of a less-favored wife and to make Joseph his heir.

Compass navigation—The KJV says that Paul and his companions "fetched a compass" when they were sailing to Rome. This is both a mistranslation and an anachronism.

Near the end of his career (as recorded in the Book of Acts), Paul was a prisoner on his way to Rome to have his appeal heard by Caesar. According to the KJV, Paul and his companions stayed in Syracuse for three days and then "fetched a compass" and came to Rhegium (Acts 28:13). The phrase has a certain quaint charm; one can almost imagine the captain of the vessel asking one of his sailors, "Fetch a compass, would you? We need to figure out which way we are sailing."

But the mention of a compass here comes more than a thousand years too early. Navigation by magnetic compass was not practiced until the 1300s. In the first century sailors would get their bearings according to islands and visible landmarks on the shore as well as by the stars. The phrase in the Greek original is not a reference to a magnetic compass or to any instrument of navigation. It says they "made a circuit"; that is, they "took the long way around" by tacking back and forth against unfavorable winds in order to reach Rhegium.

45

Creation, Date of—The Bible does not teach that the world was created in 4004 B.C. That date for creation was conjectured by James Ussher, a seventeenth-century Irish bishop. Using Old Testament genealogies and royal chronologies, Ussher developed a table of Bible history to estimate the dates of major events recorded in Scripture.

When the KJV was issued in 1611, reference editions included in their margins the dates conjectured by Ussher. Though Ussher's dates still appear in the margins of some twentieth-century editions of the Bible, modern geologists and historians have rendered his chronological estimates obsolete.

D

Deaconness—There is no such word in New Testament Greek; there is only the word for "deacon." But when that word is applied by Paul to a woman in the church, virtually every translator has tried to avoid referring to a female deacon.

The problem occurs in Romans 16:1, where Paul writes, "I commend you to Phoebe, our sister, a deacon in the church at Cenchrea." The Greek word here, *diakonos*, is translated "minister" everywhere else in the KJV, except for 1 Timothy 3:8, 12, where it is rendered as "deacon." But the one time the same Greek word refers to a woman, it is translated in the KJV as "servant."

Modern translations tend to sidestep the issue. The RSV and Phillips refer to Phoebe as a "deaconness," coining a word that does not appear in the Greek. The NIV, like the KJV, calls her a "servant," with a footnote offering the alternative "deaconness."

There seems to be some cause for suspicion here that the translators' attitudes about the role of women in the church may have influenced their word choices.

Demons vs. disease—It is sometimes said that New Testament writers did not distinguish between demonic possession and mere illness and that they equated healing with the casting out of evil spirits. But the Gospels contain numerous accounts of healings without suggestions of demonic activity and some accounts in which demon possession does not cause any physical disorder (Lk 4:31–35). The narratives of Jesus' healing ministry sometimes distinguish explicitly between cases of demon possession and bodily illness (Mk 1:32; Lk 6:17–18).

Departed saints as angels—Despite their common depiction in cartoons and popular movies, the righteous are not promoted to angelic status after death. Jesus says that those "accounted worthy" are "equal unto angels" (Lk 20:35–36), but that is not the same as saying they are angels. Angels are a separate created order in the Bible, not beings that once were human or who will someday be human.

Also, the departed saints are not depicted with wings, harps, or halos in Scripture, but then neither are angels. (*See also* ANGELS WITH HALOS; ANGELS WITH HARPS.)

Devil, Appearance of—The devil is traditionally portrayed in popular art with horns, a tail, a pointed beard, and perhaps even cloven feet. But the Bible never offers a physical description of Satan. Popular depictions of him are derived from Greek *satyrs* and other goatlike creatures from mythology.

Satan is Hebrew for "accuser, slanderer," or more generally "adversary." The word appears only once in the Old Testament as a proper name (1 Chr 21:1); the rest of the time it is used with the article: "the satan." The New Testament uses the same word, *Satan*, and also Greek *diabolos*, the source of the English words *diabolical* and *devil*. In none of these references, though, is there a physical description of the devil. He is described as a fallen angel (Lk 10:18), but it is not clear how much of his angelic appearance he might have retained.

There is nothing in the Bible to warrant the popular image of the devil with horns, a tail, a pointed beard, and cloven feet. These are all goatlike traits, derived from a merging of Judeo-Christian Satan with the Greek satyrs, mythological goat-men known for their ungovernable sexual desire and their love of disorder. Germanic goatlike fertility symbols have also merged with the modern picture of the devil.

Those who picture the devil as serpentlike or dragonlike may find more support from Scripture. Though the serpent who tempts Eve is not called Satan in Genesis, the two are associated by New Testament writers (Rom 16:20; Rv 12:9). Satan is also pictured as a dragon cast into a bottomless pit in the vision of the last judgment (Rv 12:9). But the devil is portrayed throughout the Bible as a great deceiver and beguiler (Acts 5:3, Eph 6:11), so he would not be expected to appear in some easily recognizable form. In fact, the apostle Paul warns that Satan can disguise himself as "an angel of light" (2 Cor 11:14).

Devil in hell—The devil and his minions are usually pictured in hell, where they spend their time gleefully torturing lost souls. But the idea that Satan is the present ruler of hell comes from Milton's *Paradise Lost*, not from the Bible. Many people are startled to learn that Scripture never portrays Satan in hell in the present age, but it does show him once in heaven!

The first depiction of Satan in the Bible comes in the prologue to the Book of Job. There he appears as a kind of prosecuting attorney in the court of heaven, cynically assuming that no human virtue can withstand adversity (Jb 1:6–12; 2:1–7). Later Bible references emphasize the devil's many destructive activities on earth, but none portray him or other fallen angels residing in hell.

Satan and the demons will be consigned to hell as part of the last judgment, according to the Book of Revelation (20:10; *see* Mt 25:41). When these devils are cast into hell, they will not be there as tormenters of the wicked dead; they themselves will be among the tormented.

Dives—In Luke 16, Jesus tells the parable of the rich man and the beggar who find opposite rewards after death (Lk 16:19–31). This has traditionally been called the Parable of Lazarus and Dives after the names of the beggar and the rich man. The beggar is called Lazarus in the parable (v 20), but the rich man is never named. The name given to him by tradition, Dives, means "rich" in Latin.

Dividing light and dark—The statement in the creation account that "God divided the light from the darkness" has been grievously misused to justify racial segregation.

According to Genesis 1:3–5, God created the light on the first day of creation, pronounced it good, and "divided the light from the darkness." Segregationists have argued that God thereby established a cosmic principle, the separation of light and dark, which applies to races as well as to earthly cycles.

The Hebrew word for light in this passage refers to illumination or a specific luminary. It is never used as a color, of skin or anything else. Likewise the Hebrew word for dark here signifies the absence of light, not a dark color or pigmentation.

Even without the preceding linguistic information, one senses here a particularly egregious form of biblical interpretation. Any number of outlandish ideas can be supported from Scripture if doctrine and practice are derived from loose verbal analogies without regard to meaning in context. One could just as easily advocate the segregation of fishermen from landsmen, since the Bible says God divided the waters and the dry land.

"Dividing the word of truth"—Paul's advice to Timothy about "rightly dividing the word of truth" does not refer to some preferred method of Bible study.

Paul writes to the young Timothy, "Study to shew thyself approved unto God, a workman that needeth not to be ashamed, rightly dividing the word of truth" (2 Tm 2:15). First, it should be recognized that the phrase *word of truth* does not refer to the Bible as we know it. The New Testament, of course, had not been established at the time of Paul's writing, and the Old Testament was referred to then as the "Law and the Prophets." Therefore, Paul's phrase *word of truth* cannot be taken as a clear reference to written documents.

The verb *dividing* used in the KJV to modern readers denotes a splitting apart or separating into groups. In King James English the word could also be used more

51

figuratively, meaning "to determine or distinguish." The actual Greek verb chosen by Paul combines *ortho,* "right, straight," (as in *ortho*dox and *ortho*dontist) with *tom,* "cut, sever," (as in appende*ctom*y). Literally Paul speaks of "cutting straight" or "dissecting correctly."

Modern translations have tried to clarify the ambiguous "dividing" of the KJV in two ways. Some emphasize the act of discernment with wording such as "rightly *handling* the word of truth" (RSV) or "*handling* accurately the word of truth" (NASB). Others take "ortho" as the key concept: keeping "a *straight* course with the message of the truth" (JB) or being "*straight*forward in your proclamation of the truth" (NEB).

Donkey in the triumphal entry—When Jesus entered Jerusalem to the shouts of "Hosannah," he rode on the colt of an ass (Jn 12:14). Some Bible teachers claim that this was a sign of his meekness and humility. Others argue that the donkey was a sign of kingship and honor. Both sides are partly right and partly wrong.

Some commentators observe that in ancient times secular kings rode in chariots or on horses but that Jesus chose the lowly donkey as his mount—showing that he came as one of the poor, not as one of the privileged. But Jesus allowed the people to lay palm leaves and their own garments before him (Mk 11:8), a sign of deference suitable for a king.

Yet those who argue that the donkey was associated in biblical times with kingly honor are also mistaken. Mules, not asses, were used by members of the royal family in the Old Testament (2 Sm 13:29; 1 Kgs 1:33). A mule, the offspring of a male donkey and a female

horse, stands a foot taller at the shoulder than a donkey, so it served in ancient Palestine as a distinctive
mount for someone of high standing.

The only monarch in the Old Testament described as
riding a donkey is the coming messianic king proclaimed by the prophet Zechariah:

> Rejoice greatly, O daughter of Zion!
> Shout aloud O daughter of Jerusalem!
> Lo, your king comes to you;
> triumphant and victorious is he,
> humble and riding on an ass,
> on a colt, the foal of an ass (Zec 9:9, RSV).

The messianic king is portrayed riding on a young
donkey because he is seen, not as the conqueror treading on the people, but as a champion of the poor and
the oppressed. The Gospels of Matthew and John both
quote this Old Testament prophecy in their descriptions of Jesus' triumphal entry into Jerusalem (Mt
21:4–5; Jn 12:14–15). Jesus' mount, according to the
Gospel writers, underscored his role as the messianic
ruler promised by the prophet.

Double share of Elisha—Elisha's request for a double
share of Elijah's spirit did not mean that he hoped to be
twice as great as his predecessor.

Just before Elijah was taken up to heaven, he asked
his disciple Elisha if there was anything he could do
for him. Elisha responded, "I pray you, let me inherit a
double share of your spirit" (2 Kgs 2:9, RSV). To readers
unaware of Hebrew custom, this sounds like a pre-
sumptuous request on Elisha's part. It seems to imply
that Elisha longed to be twice as mighty as his mentor.

53

But the double share is the portion of an inheritance given to the eldest son, twice as much as other progeny (Dt 21:17). Elisha was asking to be the principal heir to Elijah's prophetic work. As the succeeding verses (2 Kgs 2:10–15) make clear, his request was granted.

Dove's dung—The Bible reports that Samaria suffered extreme famine in the time of Elisha when the land was besieged by its enemies. According to 2 Kings 6:25, the shortage of food was so severe that "an ass's head was sold for fourscore pieces of silver, and the fourth part of a cab of dove's dung for five pieces of silver" (KJV). (A cab is about two quarts, so a fourth part of a cab is about a half pint.)

Even in the total absence of food, it would seem unlikely that people would turn to bird droppings to satisfy their hunger. Many commentators argue that the term used here is an idiomatic name for some sort of bean or pod which may have resembled pellets of dove's dung. A species of chick-pea still eaten in the Middle East is called by the Arabs "sparrow dung" or "dove's dung."

Modern translations vary in their handling of the term. The RSV and the NASB follow the KJV in rendering the phrase literally as "dove's dung." Others suggest instead "wild onions" (JB), "locust-beans" (NEB), or "seed pods" (NIV).

"Drink ye all of it"—At a communion service in a Baptist church some years ago, a boy of about ten got into some trouble with his mother when his tongue got stuck in the communion glass. He extracted it with a less-than-decorous slurp, explaining earnestly that there was still some grape juice left in the bottom of the glass and he merely wanted to follow the minister's instructions to "drink ye all of it."

When Jesus took the wine and told his disciples "Drink ye all of it" (Mt 26:27), the word *all* in the Greek goes with "ye" not with "it." The phrase means "all of you drink it," not "drink all of it." Jesus was inviting all of his disciples to share in drinking the Passover wine; he was not suggesting any need to drink it to the last drop.

E

Easter—There is no mention of Easter in the Bible, apart from one anachronistic reference in the KJV. The word *Easter* is certainly not from the early church; it comes from the name of the Teutonic goddess of springtime. But apart from the name, there is no record of an annual Christian celebration of Jesus' resurrection mentioned in the New Testament.

In the Western church, Easter falls each year on the first Sunday after the full moon following the vernal equinox. If that formula sounds like it was arrived at by a committee, it was.

The first-century Christians celebrated the resurrection on the first day of every week, Sunday, but they did not establish a yearly festival apart from those celebrated by the Jews. That is the reason there is no reference to such observance in the New Testament, which was completed before the holiday began to be regularly kept. (The KJV translation of *Passover* as "Easter" in Acts 12:4 is an anachronism not found in other translations.)

It is not known exactly when Christians began setting aside a special day each spring to celebrate

Christ's rising, but it was widespread enough by the early fourth century to cause a controversy throughout Christendom. Jewish Christians began celebrating Easter (not by that name) in connection with their yearly Passover festival, since they saw Christ as the fullest embodiment of the sacrificial lamb associated with Passover. Gentile Christians, however, were more concerned that the annual feast celebrating the resurrection should fall on a Sunday, their weekly day of worship, regardless of its exact correlation with Passover. Since the date of Passover is calculated according to a lunar calendar, its date and day of the week vary from year to year.

In A.D. 325, the Council of Nicaea, among its other accomplishments, developed the formula for calculating Easter still used today (except in Eastern Orthodox churches). This method insures that Easter will always fall on a Sunday and will always remain aligned with Passover. (The term "movable feast," by the way, does not refer to a holiday involving portable food; it refers to a holy day which changes dates on the calendar from year to year.)

The name *Easter* came centuries later when Christianity was adopted by the Germanic tribes of Western Europe. Easter derives from "Eostre," the Teutonic goddess of springtime and of the dawn. (Yes, that is why we call the direction of the sunrise east.)

Obviously, the Christian celebration of the resurrection merged with the Germanic celebration of springtime. The Easter bunny and Easter eggs are pagan symbols of fertility and abundance which have no original connection with the annual Christian holy day.

57

"Eating and drinking, marrying and giving in marriage"—Jesus' teaching about the judgment of Noah's generation has left some readers with the impression that there is something sinister or profane about "eating and drinking, marrying and giving in marriage."

Jesus taught his disciples to be prepared for the "coming of the Son of man," which would occur suddenly, without warning, like the flood of Noah's generation:

> For as in the days that were before the flood they were eating and drinking, marrying and giving in marriage, until the day that Noe [Noah] entered into the ark. And knew not until the flood came, and took them all away: so shall also the coming of the Son of man be (Mt 24:38–39).

Some readers have interpreted Jesus' words to mean that the contemporaries of Noah were judged because they were "eating and drinking, marrying and giving in marriage." But there is no suggestion of overindulgence in food or drink here, nor are these activities to be considered blameworthy in and of themselves. Jesus was emphasizing the point that the generation of Noah, like those of his own time, went about their daily activities without any thought of God's displeasure.

Ecclesiastes, authored by Solomon—The Old Testament Book of Ecclesiastes has traditionally been ascribed to Solomon, but he is never identified as the author in the text.

58

The author of Ecclesiastes goes by the name *Koheleth* (Eccl 1:1), a Hebrew word which means literally "the gatherer." This is usually translated as "The Preacher," one who gathers together wise sayings or one who gathers people who want to hear his wise sayings. The author seems to be drawing on Solomon's experiences and reputation, but he never identifies himself specifically with that king.

Eden, Expulsion from—Apart from misconceptions about the forbidden fruit (*See* APPLE), there are a number of other erroneous notions about the consequences of Adam and Eve's sin.

First, Adam was not himself cursed for his disobedience; rather, the ground was cursed because of him, bringing forth thorns and thistles (Gn 3:17–19).

Adam and Eve's expulsion from Eden after the fall is also explained differently from the way that many people suppose. The Genesis account does not stress the Lord's wrath or his judgment, but rather his desire to keep those with "the knowledge of good and evil" away from the Tree of Life:

> And the LORD God said, Behold, the man is become as one of us, to know good and evil: and now, lest he put forth his hand, and take also of the tree of life, and eat, and live for ever: Therefore the LORD God sent him forth from the Garden of Eden, to till the ground from whence he was taken. So he drove out the man; and he placed at the east of the garden of Eden Cherubims, and a flaming sword which turned every way, to keep [guard] the way of the tree of life" (Gn 3:22–24).

The cherubim mentioned here are not simply robed angels brandishing swords. The cherubim (no *s* needed, since the word is already plural in Hebrew) were guardian creatures with four faces looking every direction. (*See also* CHERUBS.) Also, the sword is not described as being in the hands of the cherubim. It was probably conceived as a glittering ("flaming") sword revolving in mid-air, a protection in addition to the cherubim.

Tom Burnam, in *More Misinformation,* adds one last note concerning the Eden account: "Eve is not mentioned as being expelled—only Adam. However, the next chapter has them raising Cain together, so obviously she must have accompanied him."

Elisha's curse on the children—The Second Book of Kings reports that when forty-two little children jeered at the prophet Elisha, he cursed them in the name of the Lord; soon after they were mauled by two female bears. Sunday school teachers have sometimes tried to assure their charges that these children were actually young men, the local hoodlums perhaps, but the Hebrew wording used in the passage does not support such a claim.

This curious incident in Elisha's life is briefly rehearsed in two verses:

And he went up from thence unto Beth-el: and as he was going up by the way, there came forth little children out of the city, and mocked him, and said unto him, Go up, thou bald head; go up, thou bald head. And he turned back and cursed them in the name of the LORD. And there came forth two she bears out of the wood, and tare two and forty children of them (2 Kgs 2:23–24).

The main point of the story, of course, is the sanctity of holy men and the dangers of scorning them. But readers may be shocked that "little children" should be subjected to such severe punishment for their irreverence.

The Hebrew phrase describing the lads does not encourage the idea that they were actually young men. It is true that the word translated "children" designates males, so it should probably be rendered "boys." It is also true that this word is sometimes used in the ancient world to refer to young soldiers, as we do when we talk about the "fighting boys." But such a usage is never found in the Old Testament. Even more importantly, the word for *boys* in this passage is preceded in the Hebrew by the modifier *little*. So unless Elisha was harassed by a platoon of midgets, the KJV translation is essentially correct. Modern translations support the KJV's emphasis on the youthfulness of the offenders, calling them "small boys" (RSV, NEB) or "young lads" (NASB).

Readers may wonder why the passage specifies that there were forty-two boys or why such a large group of boys was wandering around together jeering at their elders. The number forty-two may not be intended here as an actual head count. It is a figure associated in the Bible with desolation or destruction. (*See* 2 Kgs 10:14; Rv 11:2; 13:5.)

"Evening and morning"—In the opening chapter of Genesis, each day's account of the Lord's creative work ends with the same verbal refrain about the evening and the morning which made up that day. Some have supposed that the phrase is a poetic reversal which emphasizes each day's movement from disorder to order, from darkness and void to light and life.

That is an ingenious interpretation of the phrase, but an incorrect one. The Hebrew day begins at sundown, so "evening and morning" is the natural way to describe the passing of one day.

Eye for an eye, An"—The Old Testament phrase "an eye for an eye, a tooth for a tooth" connotes to most people a barbaric code of vengeance. But the phrase actually represents an ethical advance over the earlier Middle Eastern custom of the blood feud.

In cultures with no centralized authority, no police force or law courts, the main deterrent to violence is the threat of revenge by the victim's kinsmen. The greater the threat of reprisal, so the theory goes, the less likely an act of aggression. Thus, we find taunt-songs in ancient Hebrew literature about taking revenge many times over. For example, Lamech, a descendant of Cain, boasts to his wives: "I have slain a man for wounding me, a young man for striking me. If Cain is avenged sevenfold, truly Lamech seventy-sevenfold" (Gn 4:23–24, rsv). An actual example of this massive reprisal comes in Genesis 34, which reports that the sons of Jacob plundered an entire city because one of its young men had raped their sister.

Of course, if two sides pursue a policy of escalating retribution, a society is permanently beset by retaliatory violence. One thinks, for example, of the endless cycles of bloodshed associated with the custom of the *vendetta* among Mafia families in twentieth-century America. Those who become their own law must resort to primitive means of self-protection with the same violent results.

The "eye for an eye" custom, called the *lex talionis,* "law of retaliation," is intended not as a code of vengeance but as a way of curbing unlimited vengeance. Its central idea is that the punishment should fit the crime:

> He who kills a man shall be put to death. He who kills a beast shall make it good, life for life. When a man causes a disfigurement in his neighbor, as he has done it, it shall be done to him, fracture for fracture, eye for eye, tooth for tooth (Lv 24:17–20a, RSV).

Eye of a needle—Christ's teachings about the dangers of riches could be both succinct and startling. In Mark 10:25, for example, Jesus said, "It is easier for a camel to go through the eye of a needle, than for a rich man to enter into the kingdom of God." For centuries, readers have been uncomfortable with such an implacable saying, and they have tried, in the words of Paul Minear, "to make the camel smaller or the eye of the needle larger." None of these attempts to soften this hard saying of Jesus is well founded.

The most common theory is that the Eye of a Needle was the name of a low and narrow gate in Jerusalem, one through which camels could pass only with great difficulty. It is sometimes added that the only way camels could get through the gate was on their knees; the conclusion is that the only way a rich man can enter the kingdom of God is on his knees.

There are no ancient records of a Jerusalem gate, or a type of gate, called the Eye of the Needle. As a walled city, Jerusalem had few gates, and the Lion Gate and the Sheep Gate, for example, are well known from both biblical and extrabiblical sources. The notion that one of the city's gates was called the Eye of the Needle did not emerge until the Middle Ages, a suspiciously late date for such a piece of information. Besides, Mark's Gospel says that Jesus' disciples were "astonished out of measure" by his words, a reaction which would be hardly the case if he were referring to a well-known gate.

Other commentators suggest that the word *camel* in Mark 10:25 should be understood as *rope*, a similar-sounding word in Aramaic. But a rope is no easier to pass through the eye of a needle than a camel, and none of the ancient manuscripts indicate any ambiguity about the word chosen by Jesus.

Jesus' teaching about the rich man entering the kingdom of heaven is an example of *hyperbole*, a deliberate exaggeration for rhetorical effect. Jesus also spoke of the Pharisees straining out a gnat and swallowing a camel (Mt 23:24). But no one has felt the need to reinterpret this saying or to speculate that camel might have been the name for an unpalatable dish. It would seem that Jesus' warnings about the Pharisees sit more easily with most readers than his warnings about riches. (For other examples of Christ's use of hyperbole, see Mt 5:29 and 7:3.)

It should also be remembered that Jesus' teaching is about a rich man entering into the kingdom of God, which is not simply a synonym for heaven. *See* KINGDOM COME.

F

Fear of the Lord—The "fear of the Lord" is one of the most familiar phrases in the Bible, occurring, in various forms, over a hundred times in the Old Testament and nearly twenty times in the New. And the adjective *God-fearing* has become synonymous with piety. But since the word *fear* has acquired such negative connotations, it has become a commonplace that references to "fear of God" in the Bible should be understood as "reverential awe." That rendering certainly sounds less threatening to modern ears, but it may not do justice to the Bible writers' sense of a loving but fear-inspiring God.

Both in the Old Testament Hebrew and the New Testament Greek, the word *fear* in phrases like "fear of God" and "fear of the Lord" is the same one used to describe fear of one's enemies and fear of wild animals. The Old Testament writers generally believed that one could not even look upon God and live (Ex 33:20) and that even those who sought to serve God could be destroyed if they disobeyed his will (Ex 4:24–26; 2 Sm 6:7). In the New Testament one reads again how even a loving God can quickly give out harsh judgments (Acts 5:1–11).

Though the phrases *fear of God* and *fear of the Lord* in the Bible refer to reverence and to awe and not mere terror, there may be a danger in getting too comfortable with that less fearsome rendering of the Bible phrase.

Feeding of the five thousand—All four Gospel writers recount Jesus' spectacular feeding of a crowd of five thousand from a few pieces of bread and fish. Though this story certainly suggests the dynamic power of people sharing their resources with one another, it cannot be reduced to a mere example of communal giving. Jesus' feat is unequivocally reported in the Gospels as a miraculous event.

Each of the Gospels tells of Christ's miraculous feeding of a crowd of 5,000 (actually more than that—5,000 men, plus the women and children who accompanied them [Mt 14:21]). The four Gospels report the same basic sequence of events: Jesus led his disciples to a lonely place to rest, but the crowds thronged after him. Thrilled by the healings they saw and powerful teaching they heard, the crowd stayed on until the hour was late. When the disciples asked Jesus if they should send the crowd away to find food and lodging, he instructed them to feed the crowd themselves. The disciples could find only five loaves and two fishes, but when Jesus took this meager fare, blessed, and broke it there was food enough to feed the entire crowd with twelve baskets left over (Mt 14:13–21; Mk 6:30–44; Lk 9:10–17; Jn 6:1–13).

Since the mid-nineteenth century, some commentators have reconstructed the feeding of the 5,000 by reading it not as a miraculous event but as a lesson in sharing one's resources. These writers surmise that when the crowds saw Jesus and his disciples giving what little they had, they too were inspired to share. Those who had brought provisions gave a portion to those who had not so that there was enough for everyone. This interpretation allows the reader to avoid the issue of the miraculous events in the Bible (at least in this one passage), but it has little to recommend it if the Gospel accounts are to be given any credence at all.

Most obviously, the episode seems hardly worth recording in such detail if no miracle happened. The crowds themselves thought they had witnessed a miracle (Jn 6:14). In fact, John reports that crowds continued to follow Jesus simply because they were hoping for more bread. This would be odd behavior if the only bread they had received had been from their own neighbors. In addition, Jesus himself referred to the incident the next day as a miracle (Jn 6:26). He also made a direct comparison between his feeding of the crowd and the miraculous provision of manna, the bread from heaven, for the Israelites in the wilderness (Jn 6:30–38).

One must also ask why all four Gospel writers would leave out the crucial fact that the crowds had brought along enough provisions to feed themselves. Why would those who came prepared have brought so much extra when they were already in a hurry and on foot? The accounts mention that the crowds ran to meet Jesus and that the disciples themselves had not had time to eat. They include the number of loaves and fishes available, and John even specifies which disciple Jesus actually spoke to (6:5). Mark's account makes clear that the fish blessed by Jesus were the same ones

67

that all were fed by (6:41). Amid all this wealth of detail, it defies credibility that none of the writers would happen to mention several tons of food being carried by some more prudent members of the crowd.

Fiery chariot—One of the most well-known incidents in the Bible is the prophet Elijah's ride to heaven in a fiery chariot. This episode is easily one of the favorite biblical subjects of painters and illustrators, and it inspired the spiritual known and sung throughout the world, "Swing Low, Sweet Chariot."

But the Bible clearly states that Elijah was *not* carried to heaven by a fiery chariot but by a whirlwind:

> And it came to pass, as they [Elijah and Elisha] still went on, and talked, that, behold, there appeared a chariot of fire, and horses of fire, and parted them both asunder; and Elijah went up by a whirlwind into heaven (2 Kgs 2:11).

In the Old Testament, both the fiery chariot and the whirlwind are associated with the presence of God. But the fiery chariot in this passage was not sent to carry Elisha to heaven; its purpose was to separate Elijah, whose work on earth was ended, from his disciple Elisha, whose ministry was just beginning.

Firmament—The firmament mentioned in the Old Testament is not simply a poetic reference to heaven or to the skies above; it is a canopy, a structure created to separate the waters above the earth from those below.

In songs and sermons the word *firmament* is often used as a poetic archaism for "the heavens." But the term *firmament* in the Bible does not refer simply to

Elijah was carried up to heaven by a whirlwind, not by a fiery chariot.
Elijah Taken Up in a Chariot of Fire; Giovanni Battista Piazzetta;
National Gallery of Art, Washington; Samuel H. Kress Collection.

the airy expanse over our heads. It is, as its name implies, a firm thing, something needed to support the vault of the heavens. The Hebrew word translated firmament suggests something hammered out flat and broad like a metal (though scholars disagree on whether that description should be taken literally or figuratively).

The clearest description of the firmament comes in the creation story:

> And God said, Let there be a firmament in the midst of the waters, and let it divide the waters from the waters. And God made the firmament, and divided the waters which were under the firmament from the waters which were above the firmament: and it was so (Gn 1:6–7).

Note here that the firmament was placed amidst the waters. In the watery chaos that existed in the initial stage of creation, there was no separation of waters above and below. When the firmament was created, though, the primordial waters above and below were put into separate compartments. This allowed the dry land to appear once the waters under the dome of heaven were gathered into one place (Gn 1:9).

This conception of the firmament as a canopy keeping out the waters is especially evident in the flood story. Genesis 7:11 says that "In the six hundredth year of Noah's life . . . were all the fountains of the great deep broken up, and the windows of heaven were opened." This is not simply the description of a rainstorm, even a violent and prolonged rainstorm. Rather, it suggests that the waters below the firmament ("the fountains of the great deep") were surging up and that the waters above the firmament were pouring in through "the windows of heaven." The flood of Noah, then, threatened to return the earth to the condition of watery chaos that existed before God's creative work was accomplished.

Fish, as a Christian symbol—The fish as a Christian symbol can be traced back to the earliest centuries of the church. Some who see fish bumper stickers or door plaques assume that it has something to do with Jesus calling his disciples "fishers of men"; others think of the miracle of Jesus feeding the 5,000 from a single basket of loaves and fishes. But the fish symbol represents an acrostic. The word *fish* in Greek is 'ιχθύς. The five Greek letters in this word provide the first letters in the Greek phrase, 'Ιησοῦς- Χριστός θεοῦ υἱός, σωτήρ "Jesus Christ, God's Son, Savior."

Some scholars think that the fish as a symbol for Christians actually predates the acrostic, but none base the symbol on a biblical incident involving fish or fishermen.

"Fleshpots of Egypt"—When the Hebrews in the wilderness yearned for the "fleshpots of Egypt," they were not thinking about sex but about food.

The term *fleshpots* is sometimes misunderstood as a reference to sensual women. Mentioning "the flesh pots of Egypt" to a younger audience will more likely make them snicker than make their mouths water. They are probably interpreting the word as a blend of the word *sexpots* with the term *flesh* in the sense of fleshly desires.

But the context of the phrase in Exodus makes it clear which appetites the Hebrews thought were not being satisfied:

> And the whole congregation of the children of Israel murmured aginst Moses and Aaron in the wilderness: And the children of Israel said unto them, Would to God we had died by the hand of the Lord in Egypt, when we sat by the fleshpots, and when we did eat bread to the full; for ye have brought us forth into this wilderness, to kill this whole assembly with hunger" (Ex 16:2–3).

"The fool hath said in his heart there is no God"—This saying, which opens Psalm 14 and Psalm 53, should not be taken as a comment on the stupidity of atheists.

Admittedly, taken by itself, the verse seems to state unequivocally that anyone who doesn't believe in God lacks intelligence or integrity or both. But the two psalms (which are virtually identical) go on to condemn, not intellectual skepticism, but corrupt behavior. The fools described are those who follow their own evil ways while ignoring the fact that God will eventually call them to account. The fools are not questioning God's existence but simply living as if he did not exist and thereby they disregard his wrath and eventual judgment.

Old Testament writers simply assume the existence of God. They do not arrange proofs of the fact or attempt to refute skeptics—simply because the issue never arises. Even in times of great deprivation or oppression, their question is not "Does God exist?" but rather "How long, O Lord?" The modern debate about whether or not God exists is a Greek legacy; it is an issue alien to the Hebrew way of thinking.

"For unto us a child is born, unto us a son is given"

> For unto us a child is born,
> Unto us a son is given:
> And the government shall be upon his shoulder:
> And his name shall be called
> Wonderful, Counsellor, the mighty God,
> The everlasting father, the Prince of Peace (Is 9:6).

These words, borne into the hearts of millions by the libretto of Handel's *Messiah*, are taken from the prophet Isaiah's exultant vision of the future messianic king. Christians have cherished these lines throughout the centuries as a promise of the coming Christ who would redeem beyond even the prophets' imagining.

Some expositors, however, have interpreted the first two lines as a very specific foretelling of the dual nature of Jesus Christ as both God and man. They point to the double construction of the phrases, the prediction of one who would be both a child ("a child of woman") and a son ("Son of God").

Though this majestic passage certainly looks forward to one who will be both king and redeemer, the dual phrasing of the opening lines does not in itself suggest the prediction of a miraculous being with a dual nature. The double construction of the sentence is a poetic parallelism, a "thought-rhyme" in which the key idea is repeated in different words. There are literally hundreds of such thought-rhymes in the Old Testament. In fact, this sort of parallelism with repetition is the most distinctive feature of Hebrew poetry.

Another example of this dual phrasing for emphasis can be found just a few verses earlier in Isaiah's prophecy: "The people that walked in darkness have seen a great light: they that dwell in the land of the shadow of death, upon them hath the light shined" (9:2).

While Christians can quote Isaiah chapter 9 as a promise of the Messiah, they would do well not to insist that it predicts, in specific terms, a redeemer who is both God and man.

Frankincense—Properly speaking, frankincense is not itself a kind of incense but an aromatic resin sometimes added to incense.

Frankincense is best known as one of the gifts presented, along with gold and myrrh, by the Magi to the baby Jesus. Christmas pageants sometimes portray one of the Magi carrying burning incense as he comes to the stable. But that would mean he is using up his gift before presenting it to the newborn king.

Frankincense is a sweet-smelling gum from the frankincense tree, a species of terebinth found mainly in Arabia. A related European species produces the solvent turpentine (a name derived from the word *terebinth*). In the Bible, frankincense is sometimes added to incense (Ex 30:34) and sometimes used separately as a perfume (Sg 3:6).

G

Gabriel's Horn—The angel Gabriel is not identified in Scripture as the one who will blow his horn to announce the return of Christ. In fact, Gabriel is never portrayed in the Bible with a trumpet at all.

Gabriel is traditionally considered one of the archangels, though he is never identified as such in Scripture. He first appears in the Old Testament Book of Daniel to explain some of the prophet's visions of future events (Dn 8:15–27, 9:21–27). In the New Testament, Gabriel is the herald who foretells the births of John the Baptist (Lk 1:8–23) and Jesus (Lk 1:26–28).

His role as a herald for God has probably been responsible for the popular assumption that Gabriel had a trumpet. In ancient times important heralds were commonly introduced with a fanfare. For example, trumpets are often present in paintings of the annunciation (Gabriel's announcement to Mary of the coming birth of Jesus).

In Jesus' own prophecy of his second coming, he also refers to a trumpet:

> And then shall appear the sign of the Son of man in heaven; and then shall all the tribes of the earth

mourn, and they shall see the Son of man coming in the clouds of heaven with power and great glory. And he shall send his angels with a great sound of a trumpet, and they shall gather together his elect from the four winds, from one end of heaven to the other (Mt 24:30–31).

Note that the angels are not blowing trumpets in this passage, but they are sent with the sound of a trumpet. Also, Gabriel is not specifically mentioned in connection with the second coming here or anywhere else in the Bible (though an unnamed archangel is mentioned in 1 Thes 4:16).

Gad and Meni—In Isaiah 65:11, the prophet condemns his countrymen for serving pagan gods, not for serving foreign troops.

In the KJV, Isaiah upbraids his fellow Hebrews for abandoning their God:

> But ye are they that forsake the Lord, that forget my holy mountain, that prepare a table for that troop, and that furnish the drink offering unto that number (Is 65:11).

The reader may wonder who "that troop" is, who "that number" is, and why it is wrong to furnish them with food and drink. But this passage is not a reference to aiding foreign armies or other undesirables. Notice that what is offered to "that number" is not just a drink but a "drink offering," something presented to a god.

The KJV translators had difficulty with this verse because they did not know that the Hebrew words they rendered as "troop" and "number" were actually the names of two Babylonian gods, Gad and Meni. Unaware that these were to be taken as personal names, they conjectured about the meaning of the Hebrew words according to other words with similar roots.

Gad and Meni were ancient Middle Eastern gods of fortune and fate. It was not uncommon for conquered peoples in the ancient world to adopt the gods of their conquerors when they sensed that their own national gods were not as powerful as those of their enemies. But the prophets ceaselessly called the Hebrews back to the worship of the Lord by interpreting the subjugation of Israel as a sign of God's displeasure, not of his weakness.

English translations since the KJV make clear the import of this verse either by referring to these gods by name, "Gad" and "Meni" (JB), or by describing them as "Fortune" and "Destiny" (RSV).

Gates of hell—Jesus' words translated "the gates of hell" in the KJV do not refer to demonic powers but to the power of death.

After Simon Peter acknowledged Jesus as "the Christ, the Son of the living God," Jesus blessed him and responded: "Thou art Peter, and upon this rock I will build my church; and the gates of hell shall not prevail against it" (Mt 16:16, 18, KJV). The wording in the KJV has created for many readers a mental picture of the church as a besieged fortress attacked but not overcome by satanic and worldly forces.

The first thing to note is that Jesus pictured the church besieging the gates of hell, not the other way around. In an ancient city, the gate was often considered the most vulnerable spot, and as a result it bore

77

the brunt of the attack. In this verse the church is the army doing the attacking, and Jesus promised that the defenses of the enemy shall indeed be overcome.

In the original Greek, the term used in Matthew is not the gates of hell, but the gates of Hades. Hades, the Greek word for the abode of the dead, is not the same as hell. Whereas hell was specifically seen as a place of punishment and the eventual domain of Satan and his followers, Hades was a more neutral concept, simply a reference to the region of the dead. Among the Greeks, Hades was a land of silences and shades, a dark and nebulous realm which embodied much of their uncertainty about the afterlife.

In the New Testament, the word *Hades* denotes generally the grave or a kind of way-station for departed souls. Jesus pictured the church "storming the Bastille" of death, splintering its gates, and releasing its prisoners. Because of its misleading connotations, most modern translations avoid the phrase "gates of hell" by substituting instead "gates of Hades" (NASB), "gates of the underworld" (JB), or "powers of death" (RSV).

"Gentle Jesus, meek and mild"—This phrase does not come from the Bible but from the title of a popular hymn by Charles Wesley (1707–1788). Jesus did describe himself as "meek and lowly of heart" (Mt 11:29). But the adjectives *gentle, meek,* and *mild* are inadequate to capture the full personality of Jesus as revealed in the Gospel narratives.

Despite the many medieval paintings which depict Jesus as slight and almost emaciated, there is nothing in the New Testament to suggest that he was physically frail. Jesus was raised by a carpenter and probably worked that trade for many years before beginning his public ministry at about age thirty. The rigors of Jesus' itinerary during his years of ministry and his habit of going to the wilderness for prayer and meditation also suggest a person of robust constitution.

Of course, a physically rugged individual may be "meek and mild" in temperament. And one can hardly turn a page of any of the Gospels without finding an example of Jesus' compassion and tender-heartedness. Yet his excoriations of the Pharisees do not call to anyone's mind words like *gentle* or *mild*. He called them "a generation of vipers" (Mt 12:34), "hypocrites" (Mk 7:6), and offspring of the devil (Jn 8:44). No less uncompromising were his words to his disciples about the seriousness of following after him:

> Think not that I am come to send peace on earth: I came not to send peace, but a sword. For I am come to set a man at variance against his father, and the daughter against her mother . . . He that loveth father or mother more than me is not worthy of me: and he that loveth son or daughter more than me is not worthy of me (Mt 10:34, 35b, 37).

Jesus was also anything but meek in his handling of the moneychangers and the merchants in the temple area who were selling animals to be used for sacrifice. He drove out the sheep and oxen with a whip of cords, overturned the moneychangers' tables, and poured out their coins. Many scholars feel that he thus cleansed the temple not once, but twice, during his ministry. (John's Gospel reports such an event early in Jesus' ministry, while the other Gospels tell of his cleansing the temple during the week before his crucifixion [Jn 2:13–22; Mt 21:12–13; Mk 11:15–18; Lk 19:45–46].)

Plainly, Jesus could be "meek and mild" in dealing with human weakness, but he could be fierce in word and deed in opposing human evil.

"Gilding the lily"—To "gild the lily" is, of course, foolishly to adorn something which is already beautiful. This common phrase comes not from the Bible, but from the Bard.

"Gilding the lily" is an oft-quoted phrase which is itself a misquotation from Shakespeare's *The Life and Death of King John* (Act 4, scene 2, lines 11–16):

> To gild gold refined, to paint the lily,
> To throw perfume on the violet,
> To smoothe the ice, or add another hue
> Unto the rainbow, or with taper light
> To seek the beauteous eye of heaven to garnish,
> Is wasteful and ridiculous excess.

"God tempers the wind to the shorn lamb"—This homey proverb is not from the Bible but from *A Sentimental Journey* by the English author Laurence Sterne (1713–68). Sterne did not originate the proverb but translated it from the French.

Gospel writers as disciples—It is commonly assumed that the four Gospel writers—Matthew, Mark, Luke, and John—were among the original twelve disciples, those who witnessed the events they recorded firsthand. This is a half-truth. Only Matthew and John were among the original twelve.

80

In none of the four Gospels is the author explicitly identified in the text, though the internal evidences in each Gospel lend credibility to the early church traditions about authorship. The author of John's Gospel speaks as an eyewitness to Jesus' life and ministry (1:14; 19:35; 21:24–25) by identifying himself as "the disciple whom Jesus loved" (21:20). John's narrative has all the earmarks of an eyewitness account, since it specifies even incidental names (1:45; 3:1; 18:10), numbers (2:6; 21:11), and distances (5:19; 21:8) with precision.

The other Gospel writer who was one of the original twelve was Matthew, also called Levi. Matthew was a tax collector whose call to be a disciple is recorded in the three synoptic Gospels (Mt 9:9; Mk 2:14–15; Lk 5:27–29). There has been some scholarly discussion about whether or not the disciple Matthew actually wrote the Gospel bearing his name, but the content and style of the narrative seem appropriate to the disciple as described in the Gospels. In their accounts of Jesus' calling the tax collector, Mark and Luke use his former name, Levi; but Matthew's Gospel uses his apostolic name, Matthew. Also, one might expect a tax collector to take a special interest in large sums (18:24; 25:15), to present an orderly arrangement of numbers (1:17), and to provide the only account of Jesus paying his temple tax (17:24–27).

Mark was not one of the twelve disciples, though his Gospel demonstrates a thorough knowledge of the customs, language, and topography of first-century Palestine. Mark, or John Mark, was a traveling companion to both the apostle Paul (Acts 13:5) and the apostle Peter (1 Pt 5:13). According to early church tradition, Mark based his Gospel on the firsthand reminiscences of Peter himself. Commentators have noted the special prominence given to Peter in Mark's Gospel, the similarity between his account of Jesus' life and the one given by Peter (Acts 10:34–43), and the fact that Mark was with Peter during his last years in Rome (1 Pt 5:13).

Some Bible expositors contend that Mark was himself an eyewitness to many of the events he describes in his Gospel by citing the peculiar digression of Mark 14:51–52 as an example of the author's "signature." The young man who fled from Gethsemane without his robe is said by these commentators to be the author himself, recording the small part he played in the events leading up to Jesus' crucifixion.

Luke was a gentile convert and a traveling companion to Paul, who called him "the beloved physician" (Col 4:14). Luke was the author of both the Gospel of Luke and the Book of Acts. Though some of Luke's material in Acts is based on firsthand experiences with Paul (note the use of "we" in 16:10–40 and from 20:5 to the end of Acts), Luke explains in the preface to his Gospel that his narrative is a compilation of eyewitness accounts and (probably) written documents (1:1–4).

Graven image—Almost everyone recognizes "Thou shalt not make unto thee any graven image" as one of the Ten Commandments. But the follow-up questions, "What is a graven image?" and "Why did God prohibit graven images?" elicit a variety of answers. Some people guess that graven images have something to do with tombstones. Others think that graven images are those which inspire fear of God rather than love of him. (Are they thinking, perhaps, of the word *craven*?)

82

A graven image is, of course, another name for an idol, a figure which has been *engraved,* or carved, in wood or stone. The graven images of the Canaanites were likenesses of persons or animals worshiped as gods. So great was the temptation to idolatry that the Ten Commandments forbid any kind of image-making, including representations of the Lord himself. This commandment is the reason that the ark of the covenant represents no more than a mercy seat, a throne where God may dwell invisibly with no representation of the Lord himself.

Groves—The KJV reports that among the other things King Ahab did to incur the wrath of the Lord he planted a grove (1 Kgs 16:33). Readers may be puzzled by this and other negative references to groves in the Old Testament unless they consult a more recent translation. Apart from Genesis 21:33, the word rendered *groves* throughout the Old Testament in the KJV is a mistaken translation for Asherim, shrines to a Canaanite fertility goddess. The groves were actually cultic poles set up near the "high places," the altars or pillars devoted to Baal. Hebrews were warned against idolatrous worship at the groves by every religious leader and prophet from Moses to Malachi (Dt 16:21; Jgs 6:25–30; Is 17:8; Mi 5:14).

H

Hades—The polite-sounding expression "hot as hades" is not an appropriate euphemism for "hot as hell." The Greek Hades, the abode of the dead, is different from hell both in degree and in kind. *See* HELL.

Ham, Curse of—Noah's curse was not on Ham, but on Ham's son Canaan. There is nothing in the Bible to suggest that Ham was darker-skinned than his brothers or that he was the father of the Negroid race. Nonetheless, the black slave trade was justified for centuries as a consequence of the curse of Ham.

The Book of Genesis tells us that, after Noah's forty days in the ark, he became a tiller of the soil and planted a vineyard. One day, though, he became drunk from the fruit of his labors and lay naked in his tent. His son Ham saw him lying there thus exposed and told his brothers, Shem and Japheth. These sons covered their father with a garment while carefully averting their eyes from his nakedness (Gn 9:20–23). When Noah awoke, he was greatly offended that Ham had looked on his uncovered body, and he cursed the offspring of Ham—his son Canaan and all of Canaan's descendants:

> And he said, "Cursed be Canaan; a servant of servants shall he be unto his brethren." And he said, "Blessed be the Lord God of Shem; and Canaan shall be his servant. God shall enlarge Japheth, and he shall dwell in the tents of Shem; and Canaan shall be his servant" (Gn 9:25–27).

The significance of this incident remains obscure, and one wonders if there isn't some lost Hebrew idiom or custom that would explain the seriousness of Ham's offense. "Looking on one's nakedness" may describe some unnatural act here, as it does in Leviticus 20:17. In any case, it is clear that Ham himself was not cursed but rather his son Canaan. One cannot help but sense the racial implications of this curse, since Canaan was considered to be the forebear of the Canaanites, the people that the Hebrews (descendants of Shem, "Semites") were trying to drive out of the Promised Land.

The peoples descended from Ham are listed in Genesis 10; they include most notably the Egyptians and the Middle Eastern nations adjacent to them or allied with them. There is nothing in the genealogies to support the notion that Ham was the father of all dark-skinned races—or to justify the abhorrent idea, once commonplace, that black slavery was the consequence of a divinely-sanctioned curse.

Hebrews and Israelites—In modern speech the terms *Hebrews* and *Israelites* are used interchangeably to refer to the Jews of the Old Testament. In the Old Testament, though, the words are not always synonymous. 1 Samuel 14:21, for example, speaks of the "Hebrews that were with the Philistines" changing sides and joining the "Israelites that were with Saul and Jonathan." The Israelites, descendants of Israel (Jacob), were part of a larger racial group, the Hebrews, which included also the Edomites, descendants of Esau, as well as the Moabites and the Ammonites.

The name *Jews* came into usage during the Babylonian exile in reference to their homeland, Judah.

Hebrews, The Epistle to the—Many readers of the New Testament assume that the Epistle to the Hebrews was written by the apostle Paul. But the author of Hebrews is never identified in the text, and Paul is only one of many persons who have been proposed as the writer of this book.

The title given to the epistle in the KJV is "The Epistle of Paul the Apostle to the Hebrews." No such identification, however, is made in the Greek text. The author is not one of the original apostles (2:3), but he (or she) is an acquaintance of Timothy (13:23) and apparently of Christians in Rome (13:24). The author is also well versed in the Old Testament (though he or she quotes from the Septuagint, the Greek translation) and demonstrates a philosophical background and literary polish unsurpassed by any other New Testament writer.

From these and many other clues, scholars and church leaders have speculated for centuries on the authorship of the Book of Hebrews, coming up with more than a half-dozen different candidates. The style and vocabulary do not much resemble Paul's epistles, and scholars argue about whether the basic point of view is even Pauline. The early church father Tertullian ascribed the book to Barnabas, Paul's companion on his first missionary journey. Some experts have suggested others of Paul's companions such as Luke or Silas. Martin Luther conjectured that the author might be Apollos, the brilliant orator described in Acts 18:24–28. More recently it has been proposed that Hebrews was written by Aquila's wife, Priscilla, who thought it best for a woman not to identify herself as the author.

Of course, the church's confidence in the authority and inspiration of Hebrews rests on its content, not on certainty about its authorship. But the remark of Origen, the second-century Christian philosopher, remains true today: "Who wrote the Epistle to the Hebrews God only knows."

Hell—The terms *hell, Hades,* and *Sheol* are often used interchangeably, but each of these terms has its own meaning and proper usage in the Bible. The confusion is compounded by the KJV which translates all three terms in the Old and New Testaments simply as "hell."

In the Old Testament the abode of the dead is called Sheol, or the pit. This is conceived of as a place of shades and silences where humans are only vague shadows of their former selves. *Sheol* is often the equivalent to "the grave" without reference to postmortem existence or to rewards and punishments. Thus Job cries out to the Lord, "O that thou would hide me in the grave [Sheol]" (Jb 14:13), and the psalmist, approaching life's end, speaks of being "free among the dead, like the slain that lie in the grave, whom thou rememberest no more" (Ps 88:5). Sometimes Sheol is specifically associated with the punishment of the wicked

87

and seemingly with their conscious torment after death. *See*, Ps 9:17; 18:5; Jon 2:2.

The Greek word *Hades*, which means "the unseen world," is the New Testament equivalent of Sheol. It is also the abode of departed spirits, sometimes simply a word for death (Mt 16:18; Rv 1:18) and sometimes with a suggestion of torment (Lk 16:23). The usual term, though, for hell specifically described as a place of punishment for the wicked is Gehenna. Meaning "valley of Hinnom," Gehenna was the place east of Jerusalem where the Canaanites had practiced human sacrifice centuries before Jesus' time. In the New Testament era this area became the city's refuse dump, a place of continuous burning and hence an apt symbol for hell, the lake of fire.

Hellfire sermons—It is sometimes thought that Jesus preached mainly about forgiveness and brotherhood and that it was later teachers who developed doctrines of hell and judgment. But the preponderance of references in the New Testament to damnation and hellfire come from the mouth of Jesus himself.

In the Gospel of Matthew alone, Jesus' references to hell and damnation are both more numerous and more vivid than in all the New Testament epistles combined. Jesus warns of the fires of judgment more than a dozen times while referring to Gehenna specifically six more times. (*See* HELL.) Jesus refers repeatedly in Matthew to "the outer darkness," where there shall be "weeping and gnashing of teeth" (8:12, 13:42, 22:13).

Many scholars believe that Matthew's Gospel placed special emphasis on Jesus' teachings about hell, but we find equally vivid references in the other Gospels. In Mark's account Jesus describes Gehenna as a place "where the worm dieth not, and the fire is not quenched" (Mk 9:48). Luke includes Jesus' parable in which the rich man tormented in Hades cries out for even a few drops of water to cool his tongue (Lk 16:19–31).

By contrast, the references to judgment in Paul's letters are much more infrequent and subdued, usually couched in abstract terms such as "condemnation." (*See* Rom 8:1; 1 Tm 3:6.) With the possible exception of the Book of Revelation, nowhere in Scripture is damnation more frequently mentioned or more graphically depicted than in the words of Jesus.

Helpmeet—The word *helpmeet*, a helpful companion, comes from the account of Eve's creation in the Book of Genesis: "And the Lord God said, It is not good that the man should be alone; I will make him an help meet for him" (Gn 2:18). Note that "help meet" is not one word here but two. Eve is to be a "help" to Adam and one who is "meet," appropriate or suitable. This archaic use of the word *meet* still survives in the Anglican service of holy communion: "Let us give thanks unto our Lord God. It is meet and right so to do." The two words *help* and *meet* in the KJV taken together produce the mistaken coinage *helpmeet*. Since this word does not make sense to modern readers, it is often altered by folk etymology to "helpmate."

According to Genesis, Eve was created not as a "helpmeet" but as a help suitable for Adam, one who corresponded to his own kind. It should also be noted that the Hebrew word translated *help* in this passage does not simply mean *helper*, someone inferior in status. The same Hebrew word is used in the Psalms to

89

describe God himself as "a help and a shield" (Ps 115:9, 10, 11).

"He may run that readeth"—In the Book of Habakkuk, the Lord tells the prophet Habakkuk to write his vision plainly on tablets "so that he may run that readeth it" (Hb 2:2).

The concluding phrase is sometimes misquoted, though, with the verbs switched: "so that he who runneth may read." This wording suggests that Habukkuk is supposed to write his vision on some sort of billboard so that it can be read by people even as they jog by.

The correct reading, "he may run that readeth," refers instead to those who run *after* they have read the prophet's message, like royal couriers spreading the word to others.

"He that is not with me is against me"—These emphatic words of Jesus recorded in Luke's Gospel (11:23) have been quoted as a warning against indecision or half-hearted commitment. But Jesus' statement should not be applied in a careless or sweeping fashion. After all, two chapters earlier in the same Gospel, Jesus is quoted as saying, "He that is not against us is for us" (9:50).

There is no real contradiction here if the two statements are viewed in context. Interestingly, both pronouncements relate to casting out demons, but since the circumstances are opposite, Jesus' responses have an opposite emphasis.

In Luke 9, Jesus' disciples came to him saying that they saw someone casting out devils in Jesus' name, but they demanded that he stop since he was not one of the disciples. Jesus responded, "Forbid him not: for he that is not against us is for us" (vv 49–50).

In Luke 11, Jesus himself cast the demon out of a dumb man, thus giving him back his powers of speech. Those who witnessed the event were amazed, but some of them said that Jesus cast out devils by the power of Beelzebub, prince of devils. (Matthew identifies these as Pharisees in his account of the incident, Mt 12:24.) Jesus answered that no kingdom, including Beelzebub's, can stand if it is divided against itself. He also exposed the Pharisees' unbelief as a stubborn denial of the power of God, not as healthy skepticism (Lk 11:14–23). When he concluded, "He that is not with me is against me," Jesus was not referring merely to fence-sitters but to those who deny his spiritual authority even when it is dramatically demonstrated right before their eyes.

The saying in chapter 9 refers to those who are able to perform wonders in the name of Jesus. On the other hand, the more familiar saying from chapter 11 refers to those who deny Jesus even when they have seen the wonders he can perform.

Hezekiah, Book of—"He who sitteth on a tack shall surely rise again." Inane or dubious proverbs like this one are sometimes facetiously attributed to the Book of Hezekiah. There was a King Hezekiah of Judah, who figures prominently in the books of 2 Kings, 2 Chronicles, and Isaiah. But, of course, there is no book of the Bible named after him.

Hilarious Givers—One of the most familiar sayings from the New Testament is "God loveth a cheerful giver" (2 Cor 9:7)—a proverb usually accompanied by the discreet sounds of collection plates being un-stacked.

Occasionally a young pastor with a meager salary and a Greek glossary will discover that the word trans-lated "cheerful" in this verse is the Greek *hilaron*. This word comes from the same root as our words *hilarious* and *exhilarate*. This pastor is likely to share his discov-ery the following Sunday, just before the weekly offer-ing. Explaining the Greek, he will declare that his congregation should give of their resources, not be-grudgingly, not even cheerfully, but ecstatically—gid-dily grateful to give back some portion of all they have received.

This kind of error in interpretation is so common that it has a name, "the etymological fallacy," which is the error of assuming that a word's meaning resides in its origin or history rather than in its current usage. The word *nice* originally meant "ignorant, foolish" from the Latin *nescire*, "not knowing." But when peo-ple today say, "Have a nice day," they don't really mean, "Have an foolish day." As time passes, meanings evolve and take on different shadings so that knowledge of a word's origins may shed little or no light on its mean-ing in a particular context.

Horns on Moses—One of Michelangelo's masterworks is the magnificent sculpture *Moses*, which presently resides in a rather humble chapel in Rome, San Pietro in Vincoli ("St. Peter in Chains"). Visitors who stand before the *Moses* for the first time are immediately struck by its sheer massiveness. The seated Moses is over eight feet tall! Then they marvel that the delicate curls of Moses' beard, the flowing folds of his garment, and even the veins in his hands could have been chis-

Moses; Michelangelo; Bildarchiv
Foto Marburg/Art Resource, N.Y.

eled in stone. Finally, though, they can't help but notice that this imposing figure with his penetrating glare has two stubby horns protruding above his curly locks—horns more fit for a devil or a cuckold than for one of the fathers of the faith.

Michelangelo did not intend any disrespect for Moses. Rather these curious appendages grew out of the mistranslation of a Hebrew word. The Book of Exodus says that when Moses returned from his encounter with the Lord on Mount Sinai, "the skin of his face shone because he had been talking with God" (Ex 34:29, RSV). The word translated "shone" here is used three times in the chapter to describe the mystical glow on Moses' face after returning from the Lord's presence. The Hebrew word means literally "to push

93

out, radiate" and is used elsewhere to refer to sprouting of an animal's horns. Renaissance translators were unaware of any figurative uses of the word so they rendered it according to the only meaning they knew—growing horns.

Since Michelangelo's time scholars have indeed discovered that this Hebrew word can be used figuratively with the meaning "to emit rays, to shine." This is the preferable rendering here, because the phenomemon described is associated with the skin of Moses' face, not with the top or sides of his head. Also, Moses covered his face with a veil (34:33–34), not his head. The Bible says that Moses came down from Mount Sinai with a divine aura, not with bovine horns.

Hosanna—It is usually assumed that this Hebrew phrase means "Praise the Lord" or some other expression of adoration, since it is associated with Jesus' triumphal entry into Jerusalem. But *Hosanna* literally means "Save, we pray."

When Jesus came into Jerusalem the week before his crucifixion, he was greeted by multitudes laying palm leaves and garments before the donkey on which he was riding. They shouted, "Hosanna to the son of David: Blessed is he who cometh in the name of the Lord; Hosanna in the highest" (Mt 21:9).

The crowd's shout of acclaim comes from Psalm 118: "Save now, I beseech thee [*Hosanna*], O Lord! O Lord, I beseech thee, send now prosperity. Blessed be he that cometh in the name of the Lord" (vv 25–26a).

Of course, the meaning of a word or phrase is best judged in context. Psalm 118 is a hymn of adoration, and the plea "Save, we pray" is made in the assurance that God will indeed act in behalf of his people. The

"Hosannas" shouted to Jesus suggest that the crowd expected him to be a messianic king and conqueror. Their "Hosannas" were similar to "God save the king," another cry of acclaim phrased as a petitionary prayer.

Yet it remains a linguistic irony that the crowd would shout "Save, we pray!" to their hoped-for king. Later they would cry "Crucify him!" unaware that he came, according to the Gospels, not to be their ruling king but to be their dying Savior.

"A house divided against itself cannot stand"—This quotation is popularly attributed to Abraham Lincoln from a speech about the potential dissolution of the Union over the issue of slavery. Lincoln did use these words, but he was quoting from the Bible.

The original quotation is recorded in the three synoptic Gospels: Matthew, Mark, and Luke. (These three are called *synoptic* [Greek "same view"] because they give the same general survey of Jesus' life and teachings with a number of passages in common and sometimes with word-for-word agreement.) After Jesus had healed a demoniac who was both blind and mute, the Pharisees claimed that he cast out Satan by Satan's own power. Jesus answered that "Every kingdom divided against itself is brought to desolation; and every city or house divided against itself shall not stand: and if Satan cast out Satan, he is divided against himself; how then shall his kingdom stand?" (Mt 12:25–26).

Household gods—When Jacob and his family secretly fled from Laban, Jacob's wife Rachel stole her father's "images" or household gods (Gn 31:14–35). It may seem strange to find Jacob's wife clutching alien gods when he himself was a devoted worshiper of the Lord.

But in all likelihood her interest was more in her father's goods than in his gods.

These household images, called *teraphim,* are among the earliest kinds of idols found by archaeologists. They originated in domestic worship and were associated with various forms of divination. (Zec 10:2 declares their uselessness for this purpose.)

By Jacob's time, though, these images had legal as well as religious significance. The possessor of the *teraphim* was assumed to be the head of the family and the heir to the estate. Notice Rachel's complaints in verse 14 about losing her inheritance. So her interest in the gods and her father's interest in recovering them probably have as much to do with the family legacy as they do with preferred objects of worship.

"How knoweth this man letters?"—When Jesus taught in the temple, the Jews marveled, saying, "How knoweth this man letters, having never learned?" (Jn 7:15). This phrasing of their question, taken from the KJV, has caused some readers to think the Jews were amazed that Jesus could read and write because he was a carpenter's son. But they were not impressed by his literacy, but rather by his great learning. The best reading of the Greek is that they were astonished that he knew so much about the Law and the Prophets since he had never been to rabbinical school. The same word for learning occurs in Acts 26:24, where the Roman Festus cried out to the apostle Paul: "Paul, thou art beside thyself; much learning doth make thee mad."

"How are the mighty fallen"—This phrase is usually laced with sarcasm when quoted today. One hears it most often referring to some powerful or pretentious person whose misfortunes do not evoke much pity. In the Bible, though, "How are the mighty fallen" is an expression of genuine sorrow.

The phrase occurs three times in David's lament over the death of Saul and Jonathan. Even though King Saul had repeatedly sought David's life, David never ceased to recognize him as God's anointed king over Israel. And Jonathan, Saul's son, was David's closest friend; the two shared a deep bond "passing the love of women" (2 Sm 1:26). Thus, the grief was unfeigned when David declared:

> Thy glory, O Israel, is slain upon thy high places!
> How are the mighty fallen! . . .
> Saul and Jonathan, beloved and lovely!
> In life and in death they were not divided;
> they were swifter than eagles
> they were stronger than lions. . . .
> How are the mighty fallen,
> and the weapons of war perished!
> (2 Sm 1:19, 23, 27, RSV)

I

Immaculate Conception—It is frequently assumed that the term *immaculate conception* is the formal, theological name for the virgin birth. The term does not refer to the birth of Jesus but to the conception of his mother, Mary.

The Bible plainly teaches that Jesus was conceived by the Holy Spirit and born of the virgin Mary (Mt 1:18–25; Lk 1:26–35). It says nothing about the conception and birth of Mary. But Christian theologians in the twelfth century raised the argument that Mary, as the mother of God, must have been immune to original sin, or else her son, despite his moral perfection, would have been "born into sin" as a natural descendant of Adam.

Though there is no biblical foundation for this teaching, it was accepted informally for centuries until it was adopted as official dogma by the Roman Catholic Church in 1854.

Inn—Not only was there "no room in the inn" for Joseph and Mary, but there was no inn in the modern sense of the word. The words translated "inn" in the

Bible refer to lodging places in general, not to hotels as we think of them (Gn 42:27; Lk 2:7; 10:34). The inns of ancient times were called *caravansaries*, stopping-places for caravans and other travelers. A caravansary, as defined in McKenzie's *Dictionary of the Bible*, was "a large walled enclosure, open to the sky except around the inner walls, where a roof furnished shelter from sun and rain" (p. 389).

"In the beginning was the Word"—These opening words of the Gospel of John do not refer to the origins of language or to some primeval edict by God.

John begins his Gospel with a brief philosophical preface to provide a cosmic framework for the events he will describe in succeeding chapters. John wants to make it clear from the outset that Jesus of Nazareth was not simply a moral teacher or miracle-worker but also the embodiment of God in human form: "And the Word was made flesh, and dwelt among us, (and we beheld his glory, the glory as of the only begotten of the Father,) full of grace and truth" (Jn 1:14).

In his explanation of the significance of Christ's coming to earth, John adapts a term from Greek philosophy: *Logos*. The Logos, translated Word (or in some contexts Wisdom), was in Greek thought the divine utterance, the organizing principle, which gave meaning and coherence to human thought and human institutions. For John the term is used to mean the self-disclosure of God in human form, the eternal expressed in the temporal.

After his memorable opening phrase, "In the beginning was the Word," John continues: "and the Word was with God, and the Word was God" (Jn 1:1). The reference here is not to the birth of human speech or to some primordial pronouncement. It refers to God incarnated in human form for the ultimate purpose of redemption (Jn 1:1–14).

Israelis—Those who belong to the nation of Israel in the Bible may be called Jews, Hebrews, or Israelites, but not Israelis. (*See* HEBREWS AND ISRAELITES.) *Israeli*, a name from modern Hebrew, refers to an inhabitant of the Jewish state established in 1948. It is not correct to call residents of contemporary Israel "Israelites."

"It is better to lie on the belly of a whore than to spill your seed upon the ground"—Some years ago a visitor to the sailors' barracks at a large naval base was amazed one Saturday night to find a dozen sailors frantically paging through Bibles. When he asked what had inspired their dutiful searching of the Scriptures, he discovered that a young ensign had offered $50 to anyone who could find the verse, "It is better to lie on the belly of a whore than to spill your seed upon the ground." Of course, the ensign kept his money.

Some of the sailors may have been thinking about the curse on Onan, but his sin did not merely involve "spilling his seed." (*See also* ONANISM.)

"It is more blessed to give than to receive"—This is indeed one of the sayings of Jesus, but it is not found in the Beatitudes or in the Sermon on the Mount. In fact, it does not appear anywhere in the Gospels, but rather in the Book of Acts.

In Paul's farewell address to the elders of the church at Ephesus, he concludes:

100

I coveted no one's silver or gold or apparel. You your-
selves know that these hands ministered to my necessities, and to those who were with me. In all things I
have shown you that by so toiling one must help the
weak, remembering the words of the Lord Jesus, how
he said, "It is more blessed to give than to receive" (Acts
20:33–35, rsv).

Note that Paul is referring to giving of one's toil here,
not just money. The kind of blessed giving Paul has in
mind seems to involve more labor than just unfolding
one's wallet.

"I will lift up mine eyes unto the hills"—In the opening
lines of Psalm 121, the psalmist does not expect help to
come from the hills, but from the Lord.

In the kjv, this psalm of quiet reassurance begins, "I
will lift mine eyes unto the hills, from whence cometh
my help. My help cometh from the Lord, which made
heaven and earth" (Ps 121:1–2). The punctuation of the
first verse in the kjv suggests that the psalmist expects
his help to come from the hills. But then in verse two
the psalmist looks instead to the Lord for help.

This ambiguity is removed in modern translations,
where the phrase "from whence cometh my help" is
treated as a question. Thus, verse two becomes the
answer to the question posed in verse 1. In the rsv for
example, we find: "I lift up my eyes to the hills. From
whence does my help come? My help comes from the
Lord, who made heaven and earth" (Ps 121:1–2).

Among the peoples of the ancient Near East, mountains were frequently viewed as holy and sometimes
even venerated as gods in and of themselves. The Canaanite high places, shrines to local fertility gods,

101

were, as their name suggests, often located on mountaintops.

Mountains also played an important role in the religious life of Israel. Abraham showed his willingness to sacrifice Isaac atop a mountain (Gn 22:10–14), and the Lord first appeared to Moses in a burning bush at Mount Horeb (Ex 3:1–6). At the same mountain, also called Sinai, Moses later received the Ten Commandments (Ex 19, 20). In the sacred history of the Jews we also find frequent references to Mount Hermon, Mount Carmel, and Mount Zion.

But the religious leaders of the Jews repudiated the high places as expressions of idolatrous worship (Lv 26:30; Dt 33:29). The Old Testament writers consistently stressed that the mountains, as a part of God's creation, reflect his glory and majesty (Ps 90:2, 97:4–5). The psalmist in Psalm 121 may well be proclaiming that help lies not in the high places but in the Most High.

J

Jacob's ladder—The old spiritual might be better sung, "We are climbing Jacob's staircase."

Sleeping in the wilderness one night with his head resting on a pillow of stone, Jacob dreamt he saw a ladder reaching up to heaven with angels ascending and descending (Gn 28:12). Artists who have portrayed this vision seem to have trouble depicting angels ascending and descending on a wooden, runged ladder; they usually solve the problem by representing the ladder as a stone staircase. Their artistic instincts may serve them well in this case, since the Hebrew word translated "ladder" in nearly all English versions may also be understood as "staircase."

In ancient times, ladders were used primarily to scale the walls of a besieged city. Jacob's vision, however, is not one of warfare but one of serene and stately communion between heaven and earth. Some scholars believe that Jacob's dream pictures a ziggurat, a temple-pyramid like the tower of Babel, connecting heaven and earth.

The use of the word *ladder* in this passage certainly cannot be considered an error in translation, since that

Jacob's staircase.
Jacob's Dream; Vasari; Walter Art Gallery, Baltimore.

term is found in virtually every English version, both old and new. Let it suffice to say that the alternative reading "staircase" seems more befitting the context.

Jehovah—This rendering of the divine name originated by mistake in the sixteenth century and does not represent any form of the Hebrew name for God.

Ancient Hebrew writing included only the consonants of words so that the personal name for God, "Yahweh," was written as "YHWH." (This is called the *Tetragrammaton,* a Greek word meaning "four letters.") In the early Middle Ages, when Jewish scholars added vowels to the sacred texts, they did not add the vowels to YHWH, because they believed that the name was too sacred to be read aloud. Instead they added dots representing the vowels for *Adonai,* another name for God usually translated Lord.

104

Jewish cantors understood that the word *Adonai* should be substituted whenever YHWH appeared, but later uninitiated readers combined the consonants of *Yahweh* with the vowels for *Adonai*. This created the hybrid word *Jehovah*, a name for God frequently heard today but one which never existed in biblical times.

Jonah and the whale—Perhaps the most widespread biblical misconception is that Jonah was swallowed by a whale. The account of this incident in the Book of Jonah refers simply to a "great fish."

In the Book of Jonah, the Lord commanded Jonah to go east to Nineveh, the capital city of the Assyrians, to call them to repentance. Jonah set out in the exact opposite direction by boarding a ship for Tarshish, a place just about as far west as one could go in the ancient world. On the way, the ship encountered a violent storm that made the mariners fear for their lives. When the sailors drew lots to discover who was the cause of the tumult, the lot fell on Jonah, who confessed that he was trying to flee from the command of his God. He advised the sailors to cast him overboard. They finally did so in desperation, and the sea became calm again (1:1–16).

In Jonah 1:17, however, we are told that the Lord prepared a great fish to swallow Jonah. The Hebrew words clearly denote "great fish," and they are translated that way in the KJV and in modern English versions. The mammal we call a whale was probably not even known to the writers of the Old Testament.

Apart from the misinformation about the whale, the Book of Jonah is also subject to misinterpretation, because of the "fishy part" of the story. Thematically, the

105

most important part of the book comes after Jonah's ordeal in the belly of the fish.

After three days, the Lord directed the fish to vomit the prophet onto dry land. Jonah then obeyed the Lord by going to Nineveh to declare that the city would be destroyed in forty days. In a response that seemed to surprise even Jonah, the Ninevites embraced the message and repented. Then to Jonah's great annoyance, the Lord honored their repentance and spared the city (2:10–3:10).

Jonah confessed that he originally fled to Tarshish because he knew that a gracious and merciful God would not destroy the Ninevites if they repented. The story concludes with Jonah's final lesson: that the Lord loves all people, even the Assyrians whom the Jews intensely hated, and that he is not willing that any should perish without a chance to be saved (chapter 4).

The Book of Jonah, then, is a lot more than a fish story; it is about obeying God's call and about God's love for all nations, Jews and Gentiles alike.

Joseph testing his brothers—When Joseph's brothers came to Egypt for grain, his treatment of them seems to some readers to be at best capricious and at worst malicious (Gn 42–45). But Joseph was not trying to get even with those who had betrayed him earlier; rather, he wanted to see if they would be any more loyal to their brother Benjamin than they were to him.

Joseph had been his father Jacob's favorite son and the offspring of his most-beloved wife Rachel. Jealous of his preeminence in their father's heart, Joseph's half-brothers sold him to slave traders and told their father that he had been killed by a wild animal. Taken to Egypt, Joseph suffered further injustices, but his natural wisdom and his God-given ability to interpret dreams soon brought him to the attention of Pharaoh (Gn 37, 39–41).

Years later when Joseph's brothers came to Egypt seeking to buy grain during a severe famine, they did not recognize the powerful magistrate who controlled the grain distribution as the brother they had abandoned.

Joseph's behavior at this point in the story has puzzled many readers. Joseph did not reveal himself to his brothers, neither forgiving them outright nor punishing them outright. He developed an elaborate scheme which strikes some readers as devious and seemingly pointless. He accused his brothers of being spies, held one brother as surety, and demanded that they bring their youngest brother, Benjamin, back with them the next time they come for grain. This greatly troubled his brothers, for they knew that Joseph's "death" almost killed their father with grief and that Benjamin had taken Joseph's place in their father's heart, since Benjamin was his youngest son and the only other son of Rachel (Gn 42).

As the famine continued, Joseph's brothers were forced to return to Egypt for more grain. They reluctantly brought along Jacob's youngest son, Benjamin, despite their father's grave misgivings. Joseph gave them the grain, but he had his steward hide a silver cup in Benjamin's grain sack. Then he discovered the "stolen" cup and demanded that Benjamin stay in Egypt as his slave (Gn 43:1–44:17).

This is the climax of the narrative, though its significance is missed by many readers. Joseph did not develop this scheme simply to harass his brothers or to belabor his revenge. After all, he had the power to im-

107

prison them or kill them the very first time he saw them in Egypt. And Joseph is depicted throughout the Genesis account as a tender-hearted man who endured injustices without seeking retribution. The purpose of Joseph's ingenious scheme was to test his brothers, to create a situation which would reveal if they had changed since the day they sold him into slavery. He needed to know if they would forsake Benjamin, their father's favorite, the way they had forsaken him.

And his brothers had changed. Rather than abandon Benjamin when given every opportunity to do so by Joseph's scheme, they tore their garments in grief (44:13). Judah, the second eldest, made a poignant plea for Benjamin's freedom while offering himself as a slave in Benjamin's stead (44:18–34).

This was what Joseph needed to know. After Judah's eloquent entreaty, Joseph wept openly and revealed himself as their abandoned brother. He told them his story, never mentioning his forgiveness but assuming it. Only after his plan was accomplished could Joseph be restored to his father and reconciled to his brothers.

Judges—For modern readers, the term *judge* used throughout the Book of Judges evokes the mental picture of a black-robed magistrate presiding over a court of law. But the judges in the Old Testament book of that name were usually Israelite military heroes who ruled in the turbulent times between the Jews' entry into Canaan under Joshua and the establishment of the monarchy under Saul.

The Hebrew word translated *judge* means basically leader or ruler. In the context of the Book of Judges, it can probably be best translated as war leader.

The full meaning of the word is rooted in its historical context. When the Hebrews entered the Promised Land under the leadership of Joshua, they were fairly successful at first in subduing the various Canaanite peoples. After the death of Joshua, though, the Jews were less unified and less able to overcome their enemies in the region. What followed was something of a stalemate with the Israelites holding the arid hill-country and the original inhabitants clinging to the fertile coastal regions. It was a time of apostasy and internal strife among the Hebrews "when every man did that which was right in his own eyes" (Jgs 17:6).

In this time of confusion and upheaval there arose a series of Israelite champions more renowned in war than in peace. When one of these Hebrew leaders was effective against the enemies of the Israelites, he was called a judge, a nonhereditary title of authority. The most well-known of these was Samson, who settled one of his cases not with jurisprudence, but with the jawbone of an ass (Jgs 15:15).

K

"Kingdom Come"—"I'm going to blow you to Kingdom Come!" So goes the slang expression, implying that Kingdom Come refers to the next world—either the life to come after death or the world to come after this one ends. The phrase in Scripture has no such fanciful connotations.

The term is derived from the Lord's Prayer:

> Our Father who art in heaven,
> Hallowed be thy name.
> Thy kingdom come
> Thy will be done
> On earth as it is in heaven (Mt 6:9–10, RSV).

When Jesus spoke of "the kingdom," he was not using a synonym for heaven. The term *kingdom of God* (or often "kingdom of heaven" in Matthew) is, quite simply, the realm where God is recognized as King. When Jesus proclaimed that the kingdom is "at hand," he meant that God is not just "out there," that the kingdom is "within you," and that his hearers have in their own hearts the capacity to respond to God's will. Both

110

phrases carry an eschatological urgency, a sense that God has dramatically entered into the affairs of his creation.

Therefore, when Jesus prayed "Thy kingdom come, thy will be done, on earth as it is in heaven," he was asking that the Father's sovereignty, his divine will, be assented to on earth as fully as it is in heaven.

Kingdom of God vs. kingdom of heaven—In the Gospels, one encounters both the "kingdom of God" and "the kingdom of heaven." (*See* KINGDOM COME.) In times past commentators argued that the two terms were distinct, each with its own theological significance. But the two terms are synonymous and interchangeable.

It has been argued that "the kingdom of God" refers to the reign of God throughout the universe, while the "kingdom of heaven" denotes God's kingdom on earth only. But such a fine shading of difference is not borne out by the Gospel texts.

The phrase "kingdom of heaven" appears only in Matthew's Gospel in instances where Mark and Luke use "kingdom of God." The substitution of "heaven" for "God" reflects the Jewish habit of avoiding direct utterance of the name of God. (Matthew also refers to God as the "Father in heaven" fifteen times, whereas Mark uses it only once and Luke, the gentile, not at all.)

Frequently, though, the two terms are used interchangeably in the Gospels. For example, Jesus speaks of the difficulty of a rich man getting into the kingdom of heaven in Matthew 19:23, but in the next verse he speaks of how hard it is for a rich man to enter the kingdom of God. Also, in Mark's Gospel Jesus is quoted as saying, "Suffer the little children to come unto me and forbid them not: for of such is the kingdom of God" (Mk 10:14); in Matthew the words are "Suffer little children, and forbid them not, to come unto me: for of such is the kingdom of heaven" (Mt 19:14).

King James Version*—There are a number of myths surrounding the King James translation of the Bible, which will straightway be dispelled.

The KJV was not the first translation of the Bible into English and was not even among the earliest. In England, the Venerable Bede translated John's Gospel into Anglo-Saxon in the seventh century. William Tyndale produced an English translation of the New Testament in 1525, an act for which he was imprisoned and martyred. The first complete English translation of the Bible, prepared by Miles Coverdale, was issued ten years later. In the 1500s four other English versions of the Bible appeared before the King James Version (1611) established itself as the standard in English.

---

*This handbook contains a number of references to words or phrases in the KJV which are now known to have been inaccurately translated or which are translated in words that have changed in meaning over the centuries. I do not mean to suggest that the KJV is obsolete or to undervalue the work of its translators.

The KJV (1611) is a masterful translation and an enduring masterpiece of the English language. In the last century and a half, though, biblical studies have been profoundly altered by the discovery of manuscripts older than those formerly available, by the emergence of systematic textual criticism, and by archaeological discoveries which have brought to light mounds of new information about ancient Middle Eastern cultures and languages.

Since the KJV was published in 1611, the English language itself has changed as well. Words and expressions that were perfectly intelligible in the early seventeenth century have altered in meaning or have become downright incomprehensible.

Nonetheless, the KJV remains *the* classic translation of the Bible into English, one whose stately prose and apt turns of expression make several of the more recent versions pallid by comparison. The Bible excerpts quoted in this handbook are generally taken from the KJV. The RSV is used where the phrasing from the older work is misleading or obscure or where Hebrew poetry is printed in the KJV as prose.

There is no evidence that the king of England, James I, personally took part in translating the texts. Though King James was a creditable scholar and though he endorsed the idea of a new translation over the objections of Parliament, the actual task of translation was delegated to fifty-four prominent biblical scholars in Great Britain. It was by far the largest and most prestigious group ever assembled to undertake a single scholarly project.

There is also no evidence for the curious legend that William Shakespeare helped with the wording of some of the Psalms. Some have even fancied that Shakespeare left his signature in Psalm 46: the forty-sixth word of the psalm is *shake* and the word forty-sixth from the end is *spear*. What is more, Shakespeare was forty-six years old in 1610, the year in which the principal work on the KJV was completed. But all such ingenious speculation is undoubtedly much ado about nothing.

"The king's daughter is all glorious within"—Entire sermons have been devoted to the opening words of Psalm 45:13: "The king's daughter is all glorious within." But the psalmist here is praising the splendor of her outward appearance, not of her inner being.

Sermons on this verse typically suggest that one's true glory does not rest on external appearances or on accidents of birth, but on the dignity and refinement of one's inner self. That's a noble thought for status-conscious listeners, but it is not what the psalmist had in mind.

Psalm 45 celebrates the splendor and majesty of the king. Verses 9–15 describe the noble ladies of his court, probably his wives or prospective wives. The king's

113

daughter of verse 13 is not "all glorious within" her heart; rather she is "all glorious within the king's chambers." The Hebrew word translated "within" means "indoors" or "facing the inside of something." The psalmist is not regaled by the princess's inner beauty, but by the splendor of her bridal regalia, as the context makes clear: "The king's daughter is all glorious within: her clothing is of wrought gold. She shall be brought unto the king in raiment of needlework" (Ps 45:13–14a).

114

L

Last Supper—When Jesus broke the bread at the Last Supper, he compared his body to the bread, but he did not associate the *breaking* of the bread with the breaking of his own body on the cross.

The words "This is my body which is broken for you" do not appear in the best manuscripts. The preferred wording is "This is my body which is for you" (1 Cor 11:24, RSV) or "This is my body which is given for you" (Lk 22:19).

The word *broken* does not appear in any of the Gospel accounts of the Last Supper but comes from the KJV translation of 1 Corinthians 11:24. The earliest manuscripts available, agreed by scholars to be closest to the original manuscripts, do not include the word *broken;* it has been left out of modern translations. Though Jesus broke the bread to share it with his disciples, he did not attach any symbolic significance to that action. John's Gospel emphasizes that Jesus' bones were not broken on the cross, thus fulfilling the messianic prophecy (19:32–36).

Lawyers in the New Testament—Just as the judges in

the Old Testament were not judges in the modern sense of the word, so the lawyers in the New Testament were not lawyers in the modern sense.

Particularly in Luke's Gospel, Jesus is shown condemning lawyers in no uncertain terms. In chapter 11, for example, he remonstrates:

> Woe to you lawyers also! for you load men with burdens hard to bear, and you yourselves do not touch the burdens with one of your fingers. . . . Woe to you lawyers! for you have taken away the key of knowledge; you do not enter yourselves, and you hindered those who were entering" (vv 46, 52, RSV).

Lawyers have been satirized at least since the Middle Ages for thinking more about finances than about fairness. Wickedly amusing portraits of lawyers can be found in works of English masters such as Chaucer, Shakespeare, and Dickens. But the lawyers denounced by Jesus were not those who handle civil and criminal cases for a fee. Rather they were experts in the law of Moses. But these had gone far beyond the mosaic code by adding elaborate and detailed prescriptions for maintaining ritual purity—rules so exact that they excluded almost everyone but themselves as unclean.

Jesus' stern words are against religious legalists, not against lawyers in the current sense.

Lazarus as a leper—The words *lazar*, "leper," and *lazaretto*, "leper-colony," come from Lazarus, the name of the diseased beggar in Jesus' parable. But Lazarus' disease was probably not leprosy.

In Luke 16:19–31, Jesus tells a parable of the rich man and the beggar at his gate, Lazarus. According to the parable, Lazarus, covered with sores which the dogs came and licked, lay at the rich man's gate (16: 20, 21). It has been traditionally supposed that his condition was leprosy.

But if Lazarus' disease were really leprosy, he would not have been allowed to stay within the city, much less at the rich man's gate. Lepers were required to separate themselves from the community and to cry out "Unclean" as a warning to others (Lv 13:4–46). Notice that the ten lepers who approached Jesus for healing stood at a distance from him as he entered a village (Lk 17:12).

Lazarus' disease, as described by Jesus, was certainly humiliating and pitiable, but it is not accurate to make all lepers his namesakes. (*See* DIVES.)

(Incidentally, this Lazarus, the character in the parable, is not to be confused with the Lazarus whom Jesus raised from the dead [Jn 11:1–46].)

Leprosy—Most, perhaps all, of the lepers described in the Bible did not have the same disease as those who suffer from the affliction known as leprosy today.

The word *leprosy* is used in the Old Testament as a general term to describe a variety of discoloring phenomena, whether on a person's skin (Lv 13:1–43), on a garment (vv 47–59), or even on a wall (Lv 14:33–53). (These last two may have been forms of fungus or mildew.)

The symptoms of leprosy detailed in the Book of Leviticus seem to describe a number of common skin conditions including ringworm and psoriasis. Some medical experts argue that the disease now known as leprosy is not even one of those being described in Leviticus, since it does not make the skin "white as snow" (2 Kgs 5:27), and its symptoms are far more disfiguring than those mentioned.

At the least, the modern form of leprosy is only one of the many skin conditions called leprosy in the Bible, and it is not a disease that flourishes in arid climates such as the one in Palestine.

"Let us make man in our image"—According to the Book of Genesis, God paused a moment before creating humans and said, "Let us make man in our image, after our likeness" (Gn 1:26). Many interpret the use of plurals in this sentence, *us* and *our likeness*, as an early reference to the triune nature of God.

But the original readers would most likely have understood this as a "plural of majesty" like the king who refers to himself as "we." The Hebrew name for God in this verse is *Elohim*, itself a plural form. Some interpreters see the use of plurals as a suggestion of God consulting with his heavenly court, as he is pictured doing in 1 Kings 22:19–20 and Job 1:6. Either way, the plurals here do not imply that the Jews already had a concept of a triune God centuries before the doctrine of the trinity was established.

"Let your yea be yea and your nay, nay"—These words are customarily quoted in sermons about commitment, about keeping one's promises. But the context reveals that Christ's instructions, reiterated in the Epistle of James, are about vain oaths, not about the finality of decisions.

Jesus taught his disciples that people of integrity do not need to back their yes's and no's with superfluous oaths. He told them not to swear by heaven, since it is God's throne; nor by earth, since it is his footstool; nor by Jerusalem; nor by their own heads. Rather they should simply answer yes or no (Mt 5:33–37). The Epistle of James reiterates the words of Christ, saying, "Swear not, neither by heaven, neither by the earth, neither by any other oath: but let your yea be yea; and your nay, nay" (Jas 5:12).

Lilith—In the Jewish Talmud Lilith is the name of a demon of the night which was described as preferring stormy weather and desolate places. In Hebrew legend Lilith was the first wife of Adam, who refused to submit to him or to have children. She was eventually cast out of Eden and came to inhabit the region of the air.

Most of those who have heard the legend of Lilith consider her strictly an extrabiblical character, an ancient Jewish superstition. Yet Lilith does appear in the Bible once, but in a form that is concealed by most English translations.

Isaiah, chapter 34, vividly describes how the nations who are enemies of God will be utterly destroyed. Verses 11–15 picture strongholds laid waste and palaces overgrown with weeds and inhabited only by wild and exotic beasts. Among the creatures listed in this desolate place is, in Hebrew, *lilith*.

Translators have been reluctant to render this as a proper name, since its general sense is a "night creature." The KJV speaks of "the screech owl" finding a place of rest for herself, while the RSV refers to "the night hag." ("Hag" is an old name for "witch.") The NASB uses "night monster," with "Lilith" given in the margin. Only the JB allows Lilith to appear in the text itself: "Wild cats will meet hyenas there, the satyrs will call to each other, there too will Lilith take cover seeking rest. (Is 34:14, JB)

119

"The lion shall lie down with the lamb"—Isaiah, chapter 11, predicts that in the coming age of the Messiah, even the animals, predator and prey, will be at peace. Verse 6 tells of a time when "the wolf also shall dwell with the lamb, and the leopard shall lie down with the kid; and the calf and the young lion and the fatling together; and a little child shall lead them."

The common misquotation gets the general sense of the passage right, but it telescopes the three phrases into one, probably for the sake of pleasing alliteration: The lion shall lie down with the lamb. Isaiah 65:25 repeats the same idea, but again it is the wolf with the lamb, while the lion "eat[s] straw like a bullock."

"A little child shall lead them"—One hears this phrase quoted when a child, or the youngest member of a group, provides unexpected guidance or inspiration. But the verse being quoted has nothing to do with precocious children or youthful leaders.

The phrase comes from the Book of Isaiah in a passage where the prophet tells of a coming age when even the wild animals will coexist peacefully with humans and their domestic flocks: "The wolf also shall dwell with the lamb, and the leopard shall lie down with the kid; and the calf and the young lion and the fatling together; and a little child shall lead them" (Is 11:6).

From the context it is clear that the child in this verse is not leading any group of humans including older people. Nor is the child being singled out for unusual leadership qualities. Rather, the passage portrays a tranquil age when even fierce beasts of the wild can be led like livestock. The verse in Isaiah predicts a

120

time of peacefulness in wild animals, not a time of precociousness in children.

Locusts as food—Gospel accounts say that John the Baptist, the rugged forerunner of Jesus, ate locusts and wild honey during his sojourns in the desert (Mt 3:4; Mk 1:6). Some readers, repelled by such a diet, have assumed that the word *locusts* actually means "fruit of the locust tree," or the carob. In fact, carob pods are also called "St. John's bread" because of the popularity of this alternate reading. But the food of the implacable prophet was the bug, not the bean.

Locusts were indeed used for food in biblical times. They were among the clean insects declared as edible in the Mosaic law (Lv 11:22). Further, the Greek word for locust used in the Gospels, *akris*, refers only to the insect. Locusts are still eaten today by the desert nomads of the Middle East, either toasted or ground into meal.

"The Lord helps them that help themselves"—This familiar saying comes from Benjamin Franklin's *Poor Richard's Almanac*, not from the Bible. Franklin may have been remembering a similar proverb in Aesop's fable of Hercules and the Wagoner: "The gods help them that help themselves." In any case, the emphasis on self-reliance rather than God-reliance reflects Franklin's deistic leanings more than it does biblical thought.

Lord Sabaoth—One of the names for God in the Bible is Lord Sabaoth. This title appears only twice in the KJV (Rom 9:29; Jas 5:4), and it is probably better known from the words of Martin Luther's stirring

121

hymn, "A Mighty Fortress Is Our God." The second verse, translated by Frederic Henry Hedge, concludes:

> Dost ask who that may be?
> Christ Jesus, it is He
> Lord Sabaoth His name
> From age to age the same
> And he must win the battle.

Most who sing this hymn assume that Lord Sabaoth means "Lord of the Sabbath." But the whole hymn describes warfare with Satan, and it would be odd to invoke "The Lord of the Day of Rest" to do battle with the devil. Actually, Lord Sabaoth means "Lord of Hosts," that is, King of the heavenly Armies.

Lot's visitors and the men of Sodom—There have been a number of misunderstandings about the events leading up to the destruction of Sodom.

Genesis, chapter 19, recounts the events which have given Sodom its infamous reputation. Abraham's nephew Lot invited two wayfarers to lodge with him, unaware that they were angels. That night the men of Sodom gathered around Lot's house and demanded that he turn his visitors over to them so that they might violate them sexually. Lot refused and even offered his two virgin daughters to the mob instead of his guests. When the Sodomites moved forward to break down the door, though, the visiting angels struck them all blind. The angels then told Lot to take his wife and daughters out of the city, because God intended to destroy the city (Gn 19:1–15).

Neither Lot nor the men of Sodom recognized the two travelers as angels. When Lot first met the two at the city gate, he bowed low to the ground (v 1). This gesture was a sign of respect in the ancient Middle East, and was not, as some readers have supposed, a sign that Lot recognized the two as angels.

A second misunderstanding arises concerning Lot's offer of his two daughters to the men outside his house. Modern readers may interpret this as a sign of Lot's own decadence or of his utter disregard of his duties as a father. But the ancients would find it highly admirable that a man would make such a great sacrifice rather than violate his sacred obligation as a host to protect his guests.

Finally, it is unmistakably clear that the men of Sodom intended to sexually abuse Lot's two visitors. According to verse 5, the men of Sodom demanded of Lot, "Where are the men that came in to thee this night? bring them out to us, that we may know them." This Hebrew idiom for sexual intercourse is well known. Yet some writers have argued that the word *know* here may be taken at face value—that the men of Sodom simply wanted to meet the two strangers to examine their credentials. Such a willfully naive reading makes the entire account incoherent and pointless. If the men of Sodom's intentions were that innocent, Lot would not need to bolt his door against them or ask them not to behave so wickedly. And, of course, he would not need to offer them instead his two daughters, "which have not known man."

Loving one's enemies—Jesus taught that one should not only love one's neighbors, but even one's enemies: "You have heard that it was said, 'You shall love your neighbor and hate your enemy.' But I say unto you, Love your enemies and pray for those who persecute

123

you" (Mt 5:43–44). It is popularly thought that this teaching was original with Jesus and that he was contradicting an Old Testament mandate to destroy one's enemies. But there are many precedents in the Old Testament for Jesus' conciliatory emphasis.

For example, the Book of Jonah is built on the theme of loving one's enemies. Jonah was called by the Lord to go to Nineveh and prophesy its destruction. Nineveh was the capital city of the Assyrians, the hated conquerors of the Israelites who were infamous in the ancient world for their cruelty. Jonah tried to evade the Lord's command, not out of indolence or fear but because he *wanted* the Ninevites destroyed, and he didn't want them to have a chance to repent and be saved (Jon 4:2). The Lord taught Jonah that he cares not just for the Jews, but for all nations, even the enemies of the Jews (Jon 4:10–11).

In addition, some verses in the Old Testament Book of Proverbs sound as if they could have come from the mouth of Jesus himself:

> Do not rejoice when your enemy falls,
>   and let not your heart be glad when he stumbles. (24:17, RSV)

> If your enemy is hungry, give him bread to eat:
>   and if he is thirsty, give him water to drink. (25:21, RSV)

Lucifer—The name *Lucifer* has long been associated with the devil. But the biblical authority for this identification rests on a single verse, which does not refer directly to Satan at all.

124

Lucifer is Latin for "light bringer," originally a reference to the planet Venus as the morning star. The word occurs in the KJV in Isaiah, chapter 14, a passage about the destruction of Babylon. In verse 4 Isaiah specifically identifies his prophecy as a "proverb against the king of Babylon," going on to describe the king's eventual defeat and death. In verses 12–15, the prophet compares the king to the morning star, since he tries to compete with the stars in heaven:

> How art thou fallen from heaven, O Lucifer, son of the morning! how art thou cut down to the ground, which didst weaken the nations! For thou hast said in thine heart, I will ascend into heaven, I will exalt my throne above the stars of God . . . I will ascend above the heights of the clouds; I will be like the most High. Yet thou shalt be brought down to hell, to the sides of the pit.

In context, this passage describes the overreaching and blasphemous ambitions of the king of Babylon. It is not hard to see why so many interpreters view the king in these verses as a symbol for Satan himself in his futile rebellion against God. But the term *Lucifer*, replaced by "Morning star" or "Day Star" in most modern translations, is not being used specifically as a name for Satan. It is a symbol for a fallen king, who has in turn become a symbol for the fallen angel.

M

Mammon—This term used by Jesus is an ancient word for riches, not a Canaanite deity.

Jesus taught that one cannot be a servant of God while also a slave to wealth: "No man can serve two masters: for either he will hate the one, and love the other; or else he will hold to the one, and despise the other. Ye cannot serve God and mammon" (Mt 6:24). Here Jesus seems to personify mammon as a rival god; but the word, perhaps borrowed from Phoenician traders, means simply "wealth" or "gain."

John Milton, in *Paradise Lost*, portrayed Mammon as one of the fallen gods cast with Satan out of heaven (I, 679 ff.). However, there is no evidence that there actually was a Canaanite god Mammon. One finds other examples in Scripture of besetting sins personified as unholy gods. In 2 Corinthians 6:15, Paul asks his readers, "And what concord hath Christ with Belial? or what part he that believeth with an infidel?" Belial, used as a proper name here, or a synonym for Satan, means "worthlessness" or "wickedness." Note also the phrasing of Philippians 3:19: "Whose end is destruction, whose God is their belly, and whose glory is in their shame, who mind earthly things."

Man, Made in God's image—When the Bible says that man was made in God's image, it does not mean that males are created in God's image in a way that females are not.

Before completing his creation on the sixth day, God declares: Let us make man in our image, after our likeness: and let them have dominion over the fish of the sea, and over the fowl of the air, and over the cattle, and over all earth . . . (Gn 1:26a). The Hebrew word translated man in this verse is a collective noun referring to all humans. (Note the second clause: "let them have dominion . . . .") The Hebrew word is *adam*, the same as the name of the first man, but it is not used as a proper name until Genesis 4:25. In the context of Genesis, chapter 1, it is a general term for humans, male and female. In other words, the species is made in God's image, not just the male of the species.

Mansions in heaven—When Jesus told his disciples that there were mansions in his Father's house for them, he was not referring to stately edifices, but simply to dwelling-places in heaven.

On the eve before he was tried and crucified, Jesus predicted the events of the following day while offering counsel and comfort to his disciples (John, chapters 13–17). At the beginning of chapter 14, he consoled his agitated followers with these words:

> Let not your heart be troubled: ye believe in God, believe also in me. In my Father's house are many man-

127

sions: if it were not so, I would have told you. I go to
prepare a place for you (14:1–2).

On first reading, these familiar words from the KJV
seem appropriate. After all, one might expect the resi-
dences of heaven to be large and luxurious. But then
the reader must pause and wonder how "many mansions" could be built inside a "house."

The KJV translation is correct, but the meaning of
the word *mansion* has changed. In modern American
English, the word *mansion* connotes a spacious and
lordly manor house. But in King James English, the
most common meaning of *mansion* was simply
"dwelling-place" without reference to size or splendor.

When the KJV was published (1611), the plural *mansions* referred to separate chambers or abodes within a
larger building or enclosure. John Milton and John
Dryden, English poets from the same century, both
referred to mansions in hell, certainly without trying
to connote wealth or comfort. In modern British English *mansions* may still refer to a section of apart-
ments (or "flats").

Contemporary English translations avoid the now
ambiguous "mansions" by referring instead in John
14:2 to "rooms" (RSV, JB) or "dwelling-places" (NASB,
NEB).

Mary Magdalene as a prostitute—It is often assumed
that Mary Magdalene was a prostitute before becoming a follower of Jesus. It is sometimes even asserted
that the name *Magdalene* is a euphemism for harlot.
There is no evidence in Scripture to support either of
these speculations.

128

The name *Magdalene* indicates that Mary came from Magdala, a fishing village on the western shore of the Sea of Galilee. The Bible says nothing about Mary's background except that seven demons had been cast out of her, presumably by Jesus (Lk 8:2). Nowhere in the Bible, however, is sexual immorality blamed on demon possession, so there is no reason to link the two in Mary's case.

Mary Magdalene is usually associated specifically with the unnamed sinner of Luke 7:36–50, the woman who anointed Jesus' feet with precious oil and with her own tears while wiping them with her hair. But there is nothing in the text to support this assumption. An even more tenuous speculation is entertained in the film *The Greatest Story Ever Told*, where the woman taken in adultery identifies herself as Mary Magdalene. Again, there is absolutely no biblical evidence for this; neither is there any mention of Mary even being married.

Mary of Bethany as a woman of sin—It is sometimes thought that Mary of Bethany, the sister of Martha and Lazarus, was a prostitute. This misconception arises from two similar but distinct incidents that are recorded in the Gospel accounts.

The Gospels record two separate incidents in which a woman came to Jesus as he reclined at dinner, and anointed him and wiped his feet with her hair. The first incident occurred early in Jesus' ministry, while he was in Galilee (Lk 7:36–50). The woman is unnamed but described as a sinner; apparently she anointed Jesus' *feet* with the oil (v 38). The second occurrence came in the last week of Jesus' life in Bethany of Judea (Mt 26:6–13; Mk 14:3–9; Jn 12:1–8). This time the woman is identified as Mary of Bethany (Jn 11:1–2).

She anointed Jesus' *head* with oil before wiping his feet with her hair. Note that the conversations which follow the two anointings are completely different.

There is no reason, then, to equate Mary of Bethany with the "sinner" he encountered early in his ministry.

"Meat and drink"—This phrase recurs throughout the KJV and, as Tom Burnam notes, creates the impression that the ancients were unduly carnivorous. But the word *meat* in times past was a general word for food. This archaic usage is preserved in our word *mincemeat*, which seldom in modern recipes contains any minced ("chopped") meat. Generally, the ancients consumed far less meat than we do today.

Mercy seat—The lid of the ark of the covenant was a slab of solid gold called the mercy seat (Ex 25:17–22). Because of its name, this is sometimes believed to be a throne on which Aaron or some other high priest might sit. But the mercy seat was seen by the Hebrews as the place where the Lord himself was enthroned, invisibly seated above the figures of golden cherubim (v 19).

Mess of pottage—The charmingly archaic phrase "mess of pottage" does not appear in the story of Esau selling his birthright, nor is it anywhere else in the Bible.

Genesis 25:29–34 tells about Esau, the elder son of Isaac, selling his birthright to his brother Jacob. As the first son, Esau was entitled to a double share of his father's estate as well as other privileges of rank. But when Esau came in from the field one day, feeling as though he would die for lack of food, Jacob made him promise to sell his birthright before giving him any pottage.

Pottage is, of course, food prepared in a pot. The phrase *mess of pottage* appeared in the chapter headings of several English translations before the KJV, but not in the text itself. (A "mess" is a prepared dish, a serving of food. This archaic word survives in "mess hall," the military term for a dining area.)

Minor Prophets—The Minor Prophets are not so named because their work is of minor importance.

Among the latter prophets of the Old Testament are the Major Prophets—Isaiah, Jeremiah, and Ezekiel—and the Minor Prophets—the last twelve books in the Old Testament. The designations *major* (Latin, "large") and *minor* (Latin, "small," as in *miniature*) refer to the length of the prophetic books, not to their content.

Miracles in the Bible—The most well-known and often-repeated Bible stories are those involving miracles—Moses parting the sea, Joshua making the sun stand still, Daniel safe in the lions' den, and of course the many wonders performed by Jesus. This has created the impression that miracles are almost a commonplace occurrence in the Bible, in contrast to their seeming absence in the modern world. But miracles are not as frequent in Bible history as most people think.

The Bible covers roughly two thousand years of human history from the migration of Abraham approximately 2000 B.C. to the establishment of the Christian church in the first century. (The pre-Abrahamic chapters of Genesis and the vision of the end times in Revelation fall outside the scope of a regular timeline.) Within these twenty centuries, the great preponderance of reported miracles occur in single lifetimes widely separated by hundreds of years. The total "days of miracles" add up to about one-tenth of the years covered in Scripture.

Most of the celebrated miracles of Scripture occur in critical moments in the history of the nation Israel, and they are associated with a few key figures: Abraham, the patriarch; Moses and Joshua, when they led the Jews out of Egypt and into the Promised Land; Elijah and Elisha, prophets after the kingdoms were divided; Daniel during the Babylonian captivity; and finally, Jesus and his disciples.

Apart from these dramatic eruptions of miraculous activity, most of the generations who lived during biblical times had to rely on the traditions handed down to them while affirming the reality of miracles by faith, not by sight.

"Money is the root of all evil"—This oft-quoted phrase is a misquotation of the apostle Paul's words in his first letter to Timothy:

> But they that will be rich fall into temptation and a snare, and into many foolish and hurtful lusts, which drown men in destruction and perdition. For the love of money is the root of all evil: which while some coveted after, they have erred from the faith, and pierced themselves through with many sorrows (1 Tm 6:9, 10).

The discussion here is about covetousness, an addictive *love of money*, not about money as inherently evil. The passage does not even condemn the rich but rather they who will be rich at any cost. (Of course, the New Testament does contain a number of stern warnings about the grave spiritual dangers posed by wealth. *See* Mt 19:23–24; Lk 6:24; Jas 5:1–6.)

As is often true of misquotations, this one seems to reveal an underlying misconception. Sins in the Bible are seldom defined in terms of concrete *nouns*, particular things to be avoided. Rather they are described as *verbs*, actions and attitudes to be avoided—especially the misuse and abuse of things and people.

"My God, my God, why hast thou forsaken me?"— Jesus' words from the cross bespeak an agonized isolation beyond imagining: "My God, my God, why hast thou forsaken me?" (Mt 27:46b). One hardly dares to speculate about the full significance of these desolate words. However, they have an unspoken context which renders them much more than a cry of abandonment or disillusionment. The words of Jesus are identical to the opening line of Psalm 22, a passage which early readers of the Gospels certainly would have associated with the suffering of the Messiah.

Psalm 22 opens with the anguished cry, "My God, my God, why hast thou forsaken me?" (v 1). It then goes on to describe the suffering of the righteous in terms which strikingly resemble Jesus' death by crucifixion. Mention is made of those who scoff at his misplaced trust in God (v 8), of bones stretched out of their joints (v 14), of extreme thirst (v 15), of pierced hands and feet (v 16), and of the tormentors casting lots over his garment (v 18). All of these details may be found in the crucifixion accounts in the Gospels.

Psalm 22 ends with the assurance that suffering is not final and that God will not hide himself from those

133

who call on him. (vv 23–31). Those dark words spoken by Jesus cast light on the meaning of his trials—and invoke a promise of eventual triumph.

Scholars disagree about whether Christ actually quoted the words of the well-known psalm from the cross or Matthew merely choose those words to express Christ's agony. Those who believe that Jesus did not speak these actual words ask why he didn't choose a more triumphant section of the psalm to express his eventual victory. But however one interprets these words, it should be recognized that they closely echo Psalm 22.

Myrrh—Despite the reference to the "bitter perfume" of myrrh in the Christmas carol "We Three Kings," myrrh is identified in Scripture as sweet-smelling.

Myrrh was not a kind of incense; it was a fragrant balsam gum sometimes added to incense. Myrrh may be associated with bitterness in the carol because it was traditionally used in burial (*See* Jn 19:39–40). But it is also called the "oil of gladness" (Ps 45:7, 8) and sometimes associated with sexual delight (Prv 7:17; Sg 1:13). Its actual fragrance is described as "sweet-smelling" (Sg 5:5, 13), which explains why it was used as a perfume.

N

"New wine in old wineskins"—When something old is revitalized or re-energized, people are likely to speak positively of "new wine in old wineskins." However, Jesus did not recommend pouring new wine into old wineskins; rather, he cautioned against it.

When Jesus was asked why his disciples did not fast like the Pharisees and the followers of John, he answered with two brief illustrations:

> No one sews a piece of unshrunk cloth on an old garment; if he does, the patch tears away from it, the new from the old, and a worse tear is made. And no one puts new wine into old wineskins; if he does, the wine will burst the skins, and the wine is lost, and so are the skins; but new wine is for fresh skins." (Mk 2:21–22, RSV)

As Jesus knew, new wine gives off vapors as it mellows, so it must be placed in a new, unstretched wineskin.

Both parables show the futility of treating something new as if it is no different from the old. In response to the question about fasting, Jesus suggested that his teaching could be assimilated into the old habits of defining righteousness according to ritual niceties. Jesus said that one shouldn't try to force his words into the legalistic traditions of the Pharisees any more than one would pour "new wine into old wineskins."

Noah gathering the animals two by two—Readers familiar with the story of Noah in Genesis recall that he gathered the animals two by two into the ark. He took a pair of each kind, male and female, so that the earth could be replenished after the flood waters receded. But the account actually states that Noah took a pair of each of the unclean animals. Of the clean animals and the birds, he gathered seven pairs, presumably taking the extras to be offered as sacrificial offerings (Gn 7:1–3).

Furthermore, we needn't wonder how Noah managed to round up pairs of all the animals of the earth. The Genesis account states that Noah and his family boarded the ark first, and then all the animals "went two and two unto Noah into the ark" (7:9).

Noah's ark—Bible illustrators usually depict Noah's ark as a wooden ocean liner with a steep gangplank leading to a deck high above the ground. But the dimensions of the ark given in Genesis describe a long, low barge which would barely rise above the water line.

When God told Noah he was going to send a great flood, he instructed Noah to build an ark 300 cubits long, fifty cubits wide, and thirty cubits high (Gn 6:15). A cubit is the length from a man's elbow to the end of his fingers, about eighteen inches. This measurement would make the ark 450 feet long, seventy-five feet

Noah's Ark

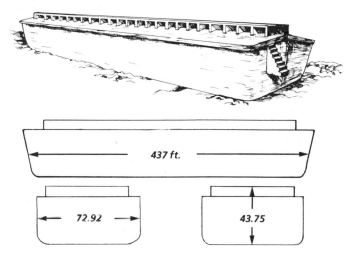

437 ft.

72.92

43.75

Volume: 1,396,000 cu. ft.
Gross tonnage: 13,960 tn.

wide, and forty-five feet high. Noah's ark, then, was one-sixth as wide as it was long, and one-tenth as high as it was long. Fully loaded, such a craft would barely be visible above the water line.

The ark, as described in Genesis, was not a ship in the usual sense. In the water it would look something like a gigantic grandfather clock floating on its back. No mention is made of sails or rudder, probably because there was nowhere to steer to in a world without land.

O

Occupation of Jesus—In the KJV, Jesus is referred to by his countrymen as a carpenter (Mk 6:3) and the son of a carpenter (Mt 13:55). Some Bible teachers, however, observing how little wood there is to be found in modern-day Israel, speculate that Jesus was really a stonemason by trade. These commentators argue that someone called a "builder" in a land of wood houses would be a carpenter but that a "builder" in a land of stone houses, like Palestine, would be a mason.

This is intriguing speculation, but it is not supported by the Greek text. Scholars have traditionally agreed that the Greek word used to describe Jesus' trade is not the general word for builder, but the specific word for a craftsman in wood. Though there has been some recent discussion about that interpretation, all modern English translations reaffirm the KJV's designation of Jesus as a carpenter.

Though wood was always scarce in Israel, carpenters plied their trade there throughout biblical times. The Old Testament mentions workers in wood specifically (1 Chr 22:15) and refers to a number of tools still used by carpenters today: axes (Dt 19:5), mallets

(Jer 10:4), plumb lines (Is 44:13), and chisels (Is 44:13).

Offerings of Cain and Abel—The Bible says that Cain killed his brother Abel after the Lord had regarded Abel's offering and not regarded Cain's. It does *not* say that Abel's offering was more acceptable because it was an animal sacrifice involving the shedding of blood.

According to the Book of Genesis, Cain was a "tiller of the ground" who brought as an offering "the fruits of the ground"; Abel, his younger brother, was a "keeper of sheep" who brought an offering of "the firstlings of the flock." The Lord "had respect" for Abel and his offering but "had not respect" for Cain and his offering (Gn 4:2–4).

This passage doesn't explain why the Lord received one offering and not the other. Many commentators, emphasizing the importance of blood sacrifice for atonement in the Judeo-Christian tradition, have assumed that Cain's offering was disregarded because it did not involve the shedding of blood. But grain and vegetable offerings were as much in accord with Jewish law and custom as animal offerings (Lv 2:1–16). So there is no obvious ceremonial reason why Cain's sacrifice would be unacceptable.

Other commentators who speculate on this passage focus on the difference between the characters of Cain and Abel, not the difference between their offerings. Certainly, that Cain would kill his innocent brother out of jealousy for the Lord's favor bespeaks a cankered soul. And Abel is remembered in the New Testament as a righteous martyr and an exemplar of faith (Mt 23:35, Heb 11:4).

139

Still others note that the Lord cursed the ground after the disobedience of Cain's father, Adam (Gn 3:17–19). Cain offered "the fruit of the ground" to the Lord, but perhaps that ground was still under God's curse, a curse not removed until the time of Noah (Gn 9:1–2).

Incidentally, illustrators sometimes portray Cain slaying Abel with the jawbone of an ass. No mention of a murder weapon is made in the Genesis account.

Onanism—Onanism is an archaic synonym for masturbation and is named after the biblical character Onan. Onan did "spill his seed," but his sin was not simply sexual impropriety. Rather, it was his refusal to impregnate his brother's widow so that she could have offspring.

According to the Jewish custom called "levirate marriage," a man's widow could lie with her deceased husband's brother so that she could raise a son to perpetuate the family name and receive the inheritance. As the Genesis account makes clear, Onan refused to accept this obligation:

> And Judah said unto Onan, Go in unto thy brother's wife, and marry her, and raise up seed to thy brother. And Onan knew that the seed should not be his; and it came to pass, when he went in unto his brother's wife, that he spilled it on the ground, lest that he should give seed to his brother (Gn 38:8–9).

As this passage makes clear, Onan's fatal sin was not a sexual one, but rather his refusal to provide a male heir for his brother's widow.

"Opposition of science"—In the intense, and frequently misguided, debates between faith and science, partisans for the former quote Paul's advice in his letter to Timothy:

> O Timothy, keep to that which is committed to thy trust, avoid profane and vain babblings, and oppositions of science falsely so called: which some professing have erred concerning the faith (1 Tm 6:20–21a).

The word translated *science* in the KJV is the Greek *gnosis*, "knowledge." In its original derivation from Latin, the word *science* also means simply "knowledge." The modern definition of science as a body of information derived from systematic inquiry did not come into common use until the nineteenth century.

Paul's warning to Timothy probably refers to the Gnostics, a heretical sect who sought salvation through inner knowledge, not through faith in Christ's atoning work. It is anachronistic to apply Paul's words to the empirical sciences of the present day.

P

Patience of Job—Though "the patience of Job" has become a proverbial phrase, Job is not presented in the Bible as a man of unlimited patience. Several times in the Book of Job, the man renowned for his resignation loses his patience, not only with his "comforters" but seemingly with God himself.

Job's reputation for patience rests largely on his initial response to the great calamities which befall him. After hearing that he had lost his cattle, his servants, and even his sons and daughters, Job answered with grave resignation: "Naked I came from my mother's womb, and naked shall I return; the Lord gave, and the Lord has taken away; blessed be the name of the Lord" (Jb 1:21, rsv). Even when covered with loathsome sores and told by his wife to curse God and die, Job's answer was a model of noble longsuffering: "Shall we receive good at the hand of God, and shall we not receive evil?" (Jb 2:10, rsv)

Yet Job was able to bear misfortune, grief, and disease better than the "comforts" of his friends. Though their approaches were different, Job's "comforters" all assumed that he was guilty of some great and secret

142

sin, for which God was exacting an agonizing punishment. The more Job denied any wrongdoing, the more vehemently they denounced him.

Some people who have heard of the "patience of Job" without ever reading the Book of Job assume that he was something of a "noodle," who listened to smug, self-serving accusations with a spiritless passivity. But early on, Job reproached his friends for their callousness, inconsistency, and fear for their own security (Jb 6:14–21). As their condemnation became more shrill and more pompous, Job lashed back in what can only be described as a burst of impatience:

> Lo, my eye has seen all this,
> my ear has heard and understood it.
> What you know, I also know;
> I am not inferior to you.
> But I would speak to the Almighty,
> And I desire to argue my case with God.
> As for you, you whitewash with lies;
> worthless physicians are you all. . . .
> Your maxims are proverbs of ashes,
> Your defenses are defenses of clay (Jb 13:1–4, 12, RSV).

It might be argued that this is only righteous indignation toward unjust friends and that Job's reputation for patience rests on his unceasing faith in the justice and mercy of God. But again one finds evidence otherwise. Job insisted on his innocence throughout his trials and cried out to God to vindicate him and to explain the reason for his suffering. With no relief in sight, Job's complaints eventually concerned not only his friends but also his Lord. In chapter 9, he said that God "multiplies [his] wounds without cause" (v 17) and wondered if God's rule on earth is at all just:

143

> It is all one; therefore I say,
> he destroys both the blameless and the wicked.
> When disaster brings sudden death,
> he mocks at the calamity of the innocent.
> The earth is given into the hands of the wicked;
> he covers the faces of its judges—
> if it is not he, who then is it? (vv 22–24, RSV).

As this and similar passages reveal, glib references to the "patience of Job" do not do justice to this book of the Bible. There we find a genuine tension between trusting God and questioning him, a very human response to prolonged pain.

Peace offerings—Many people who read of peace offerings in the Old Testament assume that they were given to placate God by those who had violated his commands. But peace offerings in the Bible were most commonly given in praise and thanksgiving, not in fear of divine wrath.

Among some American Indian tribes, peace offerings were exchanged as a covenant of friendship, either to maintain peaceful relations or to signify an end to hostilities. A variation of this custom is still common today, especially in households where occasional trips to the florist may be necessary to insure the domestic tranquility.

But the modern meaning of peace offering as "a gift to smooth over differences" has led readers to misconstrue the nature of peace offerings in the Old Testament. In Hebrew custom, peace offerings were unblemished animals burned as sacrifices and presented to God in celebration and gratitude. The meat from the sacrifice was sometimes shared with the

Saint Peter; Marco Zoppo; National Gallery of Art, Washington; Samuel H. Kress Collection.

priests and sometimes with other worshipers as a re-affirmation of the covenant relationship with God and with others.

Peace offerings were sometimes sacrificed to formalize a reconciliation between quarreling parties, but, even then, the gift was offered to God, not to the aggrieved party. (*See* Gn 31:43–55.)

Peter as the gatekeeper of heaven—In popular cartoons and jokes, recently departed souls invariably find themselves standing in front of St. Peter as they anxiously wait to discover their eternal destinies. This picture of Peter as the gatekeeper of heaven is based on confused or fanciful interpretations of Jesus' promise to give Peter the keys to the kingdom.

When Jesus asked his disciples who they thought he was, Peter answered with characteristic directness, "Thou art the Christ, the Son of the living God" (Mt

145

16:16). Jesus responded with an extraordinary benediction, saying that upon the rock of Peter he would build his church, and adding: "And I will give unto thee the keys of the kingdom of heaven: and whatsoever thou shalt bind on earth shall be bound in heaven: and whatsoever thou shalt loose on earth shall be loosed in heaven" (v 19).

From this verse comes the popular notion that Peter stands at the gate of heaven and decides who may enter and who may not. But the "kingdom of heaven" is not the same as "heaven." It is a term used in Matthew as an alternative to "kingdom of God," the realm of all who acknowledge God as king both in heaven and on earth. (*See* KINGDOM COME.) Therefore, Peter is not being offered the keys to heaven itself.

Keys in Scripture are an emblem of authority (Is 22:22; Rv 3:7), and Peter is given the authority to bind and to loose. In the rabbinical teaching of Jesus' time, these words were used to mean "forbid" and "permit." It should be observed, though, that the verse says *what*soever is bound and loosed, not *who*soever. This suggests that Peter's power is not over people.

Centuries of debate have not resolved just which powers are being conferred on Peter in this verse, but it is important to note that the same powers of binding and loosing are given to *all* the disciples in Matthew 18:18 (with the same wording used in the verse above). Scholars agree, though, that this verse does not refer to any special privilege given to Peter to determine the eternal fate of souls.

Peter's cursing—When Peter began "to curse and to swear" denying that he ever knew Jesus, he was not yelling profanities to prove he was unreligious. Rather

146

he was (falsely) taking an oath that he was telling the truth.

On the night Jesus was arrested, Peter was asked twice if he was one of the disciples, and he denied it both times. The third time he was questioned, "he began to curse and to swear, saying, I know not this man of whom you speak" (Mk 14:71). The KJV translation adds the verb *saying* here as an interpolation, but this intended clarification actually obscures the meaning of the sentence for modern readers. Peter was not swearing like a sailor or uttering profanities in the modern sense of that term. Rather, he was saying something like, "I swear to God I never knew the man" or "Let me be accursed if I ever followed Jesus." The RSV presents Peter's response more clearly for today's readers: "But he began to invoke a curse on himself and to swear, 'I do not know this man of whom you speak.'"

Philistines as vulgar—In modern usage, a "philistine" is someone who is narrow-minded, conventional, unable to appreciate art and culture. These connotations do not come from any description of the Philistines in the Bible, but from Matthew Arnold, the nineteenth-century British poet and essayist.

In the Old Testament, the Philistines were a non-Semitic people who inhabited the coastal regions of Palestine. They were perennial enemies of the Israelites, and the two nations were perpetually at war. Samson's greatest feats of combat came in battles against the Philistines (Jgs 13–16), and the giant Goliath, slain by David, was also a Philistine (1 Sm 21:9).

In *Culture and Anarchy* (1868), Matthew Arnold adapted the name *philistine* for his own purposes. Just

147

as the biblical Philistines were inveterate enemies of the Jews, Arnold spoke of modern-day philistines as inveterate enemies of learning and culture. Arnold's philistines were those so bound up in a narrow piety and a narrow practicality that they never learned to appreciate anything outside their own circumscribed world. The biblical Philistines, on the other hand, may have been guilty of massacre and mayhem, but no one ever accused them of being "too middle-class."

Plucking corn on the Sabbath—When the disciples, passing through a grainfield one Sabbath day, pulled off some heads of grain to eat, they greatly offended the Pharisees. The disciples' crime was not stealing, however, but rather "working" on the Sabbath (Mk 2:23–28).

Jewish law permitted wayfarers to pluck grain along the way with their hands—not with any kind of harvesting tool (Dt 23:25). When they rubbed the grains in their hands to separate the kernels from the chaff, the disciples were "threshing," hence doing work on the Sabbath. It was this kind of legalistic technicality in the Pharisees' religion that made them the objects of Jesus' vehement condemnation.

The KJV refers to the disciples "plucking corn" on the Sabbath. *Corn* is an obsolete English word used to refer to grains in general. The corn on the cob familiar to us today was unknown to both the biblical writers and to the KJV translators.

Premarital sex as permissible—Occasionally one hears that the Bible explicitly forbids extramarital sex (adultery) but is silent on the subject of premarital sex. This is simply not the case.

According to Old Testament law, a young woman who was found on her wedding night to be without "the tokens of virginity" could be stoned to death (Dt 32:13–22). In the New Testament there are a number of explicit prohibitions against fornication, or sexual immorality (Mt 15:19, 1 Cor 6:9).

It has been argued, though, that the Greek word translated as "fornication" in the KJV is just another word for adultery, or extramarital sex. That word is *porneia* from the same root as the modern English word *pornography*. *Porneia*, a general word for sexual lawlessness, means literally "playing the harlot." Obviously, harlots are condemned in the Bible for sexual sin in general, not for being unfaithful to their mates.

In the verses mentioned above, Jesus and the apostle Paul both list "adultery" and "fornication" separately in their list of unrighteous acts. The Bible's teaching on premarital sex may not be popular in some circles, but it is not ambiguous.

"Pride goeth before a fall"—The familiar saying is a slightly abbreviated version of Proverbs 16:18: "Pride goeth before destruction, and an haughty spirit before a fall."

"Prince of the power of the air"—A few years ago when a new Christian television station began broadcasting, one of the pastors on hand for its inauguration proclaimed that the time had come for television to be used as the Lord's medium, not the devil's. He concluded that "the prince of the power of the air" would surely bless the station's efforts to combat unrighteousness.

This phrase, which sounds like an archaic title for the chairman of the FCC, is taken from the Book of Ephesians. The apostle Paul, writing to the Christians at Ephesus, uses the phrase when describing the former sinful lives from which they have been redeemed: "In time past ye walked according to the course of this world, according to the prince of the power of the air, the spirit that now worketh in the children of disobedience" (Eph 2:2).

As this context makes clear, "the prince of the power of the air" is not a title for Christ or any celestial being. Rather, the term refers to the one whom the preacher complained about as having too much influence on television viewers already!

Prophecy as foretelling—There certainly is a predictive element in Bible prophecy, but the prophets conceived of themselves primarily as "forth tellers," giving forth the message of the Lord with moral urgency, not just foretellers, diviners of the future.

Many of the popular books on Bible prophets treat them as soothsayers or crystal ball gazers intent on foretelling the future merely to gratify curiosity about days to come. However, the prophets without exception addressed the chronic moral and spiritual issues of their own time by warning about idolatry and immorality, about oppression of the poor and unprotected, about spiritual complacency amid plenty.

When the prophets offered predictions, it was nearly always in the context of future judgment for present depravity or future restoration and peace for those presently oppressed. Though it is fascinating to study how many of the predictions made by the prophets were fulfilled by subsequent events, only a small fraction of the prophets' writings concern predictions about the future.

Psalms of David—The Book of Psalms is sometimes loosely referred to as "the Psalms of David." But less than half of the individual psalms are associated with his name.

Of the 150 psalms collected in the Psalter, seventy-one are specifically associated with David in the text. However, these superscriptions were added after the original psalms, and their meaning is not always clear. "A Psalm of David" may mean "a psalm composed by David," but it may also mean "a psalm about David" or "a psalm in the spirit of those David composed."

The psalms not associated with David seem to have been written by priestly musicians such as ten by "the sons of Korah," and ten by "Asaph." Two psalms are associated with Solomon (72, 127), one with Moses (90), and one with Ethan (88). The fifteen psalms labeled "Songs of Ascent" may have been sung on pilgrimages to Jerusalem. The remaining psalms are untitled.

Q

Queen of Sheba—The Queen of Sheba's name is usually linked with King Solomon, and sometimes it is supposed that the two were lovers. But there is nothing in the Bible about a romantic relationship between Solomon and Sheba.

1 Kings 10:1–13 describes the Queen of Sheba's visit to Israel. Having heard of Solomon's wisdom, the queen came to Jerusalem to test him with difficult questions and to see for herself if his court was as resplendent as rumors described it. She was satisfied on both accounts, since she praised Solomon for his wise counsel and for the splendor of his palace. She then exchanged precious gifts with Solomon and returned to her homeland in southern Arabia. And that is where the story ends.

The Queen of Sheba is sometimes confused with Bathsheba, the wife of Uriah the Hittite. King David seduced Bathsheba and then married her after arranging for Uriah's death in battle. Bathsheba was the mother of Solomon (2 Sm 11:2–12:24).

Quo Vadis?—The title of Henryk Sienkiewicz's celebrated novel does not come from the words of Christ or any phrase recorded in Scripture. The question *Quo vadis?*, Latin for "Where are you going?" originates in a climactic scene near the end of the story.

Quo Vadis? was a best-seller at the turn of the century, and it helped its Polish-born author win the Nobel Prize in 1905. *Quo Vadis?* portrays the decline of pagan Rome and the rise of Christianity under the savage persecution of Nero. After the mad emperor had all but obliterated the church in Rome, the apostle Peter, old, careworn, and nearly defeated, was persuaded to flee from Rome to spare his life. On the road leading away from the city, though, Peter encountered Jesus Christ in a vision. *Quo vadis, Domine?*, Peter asked, "Where are you going, Lord?" Jesus answered that he was going to Rome to be crucified again, since Peter's life's work would come to naught if he left his few scattered followers behind.

When Peter turned around, his companions, who had not seen the vision, asked him as well, *"Quo vadis?"* "To Rome," he replied, to his last days of ministry and his martyrdom. But, of course, Peter also went to finish what he had begun, to nurture a church which would long outlive the empire.

R

Rahab the harlot—The woman of Jericho who aided Joshua's spies was not simply an innkeeper. Though some translators have tried to rehabilitate her, the Hebrew word used to describe Rahab plainly denotes a harlot.

Before Joshua laid siege to the city of Jericho, he sent two spies to reconnoiter. The men lodged at the house of a prostitute named Rahab (Jos 2:1). When the king of Jericho found out about the spies, Rahab hid them in exchange for a promise that she and her family would be spared when the Israelites succeeded in taking the city.

Once the walls of Jericho "came a-tumbling down," the Israelites were as good as their word. Though the city was razed, Rahab's house, identified by a scarlet cord she tied in the window, was left untouched (Jos 6:22–25).

Since Rahab provided lodging for the two spies, Josephus, the first-century Jewish historian, and others have described Rahab as an innkeeper. But the Hebrew word used in the narrative clearly refers to a prostitute.

Rahab, the woman of Jericho, should not be confused with another Rahab, the mythological monster sometimes used as a metaphor for powers of Egypt (Ps 87:4; Is 51:9).

Rainbow of Noah—After the flood, the Lord made a covenant of peace with Noah and set his bow in the clouds as a sign (Gn 9:13–15). We usually assume this was a rainbow, a colorful and radiant emblem of God's promise. But the rainbow in this context has more somber connotations: it was God's war-bow, which he no longer intended to use against humans.

The Hebrew word used in Genesis, chapter 9, is not specifically *rainbow*, but simply *bow*. Despite the many colors, this is not the kind of bow that might top a present. It is the same word used as the quiver and *bow* that Esau took to go hunting (Gn 27:3) and the sword and *bow* that Jacob said he used against the Amorites (Gn 48:22). For God to set his bow in the cloud (Gn 3:19) means that he has laid it aside and no longer intends to make war on his human creations.

Rain on the just and on the unjust—Nowadays the proverb, "It rains on the just and on the unjust," suggests that all people, good and bad alike, must endure the vicissitudes and misfortunes of life. In the Bible, though, the sense of this saying is just the reverse; rain is taken to be a sign of good fortune, not bad.

The phrase comes from the passage in Matthew's Gospel traditionally called the Sermon on the Mount:

> Love your enemies, bless them that curse you, do good to them that hate you; . . . That ye may be children of your Father which is in heaven: for he maketh

155

his sun to rise on the evil and on the good, and sendeth
rain on the just and on the unjust (Mt 5:44a, 45).

Obviously, the context here is blessing others, and
doing good to them, regardless of their merits. In an
arid agricultural region like Palestine, rain is associated with showers of blessing (Ez 34:26), not with
spoiled picnics or flooded basements. (*See* Am 4:7–8.)

Red Sea, Parting of—The waters parted by the power
of God through the hand of Moses were almost certainly not the Red Sea as we know it, but rather the Sea
of Reeds north of the Gulf of Suez.

Exodus 14 recounts the miraculous delivery of the
Israelites from the armies of Pharaoh. Moses led his
people westward to the site of the modern Suez Canal.
When Pharaoh decided to give chase with his chariots
and horsemen, the Israelites were trapped between the
approaching armies and the sea. But when Moses
stretched out his hand over the sea, as instructed by
the Lord, a strong east wind blew all night, creating a
corridor of dry land. The Israelites crossed safely over.
When the Egyptians tried to follow, their horses and
chariots became trapped in the mire and the returning
waters inundated them.

The Egyptian fortress towns mentioned in the narrative (Etham, 13:20, and Pihahiroth, 14:2), suggest
that the Israelites' escape route was the main military
highway to Canaan. Though scholars disagree about
the exact site of the crossing, the Hebrew word for the
body of water involved, the "Sea of Reeds," and the
location of the fortress towns mentioned favor a location north of the present Red Sea in the shallow waters
north of the Gulf of Suez.

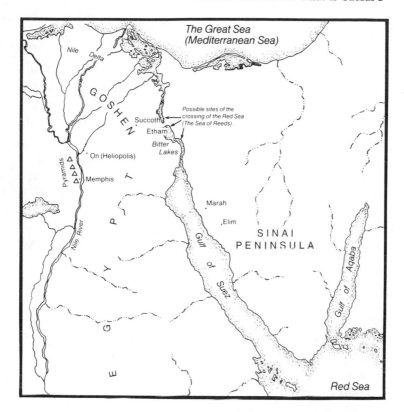

"Render unto Caesar what is Caesar's"—Jesus' answer to the Pharisees about paying taxes to Caesar is sometimes taken to be a clever evasion of the issue they put before him. But his answer is a straightforward one: both God and government deserve their due.

According to the Gospels, the Pharisees sought to "entangle [Jesus] in his talk" by posing questions that admitted no satisfactory answer (Mt 22:15–22; *see also* Mk 12:13–17, Lk 20:20–26). Hoping to entrap Jesus, they asked him, "Is it lawful to give tribute unto Cae-

157

sar, or not?" (v 17). Their question concerned the annual poll tax levied by the Romans and hated by the Jews. If Jesus answered yes, they surmised, he would lose favor with the people; but if he answered no, his enemies would have evidence that he denied the authority of the Romans and was a potentially subversive force.

Jesus answered by asking to see one of the coins used to pay the tax. When one was produced, it had stamped on it the image and superscription of Caesar. This probably embarrassed the Pharisees by reminding them that they had already acknowledged the authority of Caesar, since his rule extended as far as his coins were circulated.

Jesus concluded, "Render therefore unto Caesar the things which are Caesar's; and unto God the things that are God's" (v 21). This answer did not evade the dilemma posed by the Pharisees but met it head-on. By saying that both God and Caesar deserved their due, Jesus was saying that the tribute should be paid to Caesar and that tribute should also be paid to God. The kingdom of God, according to Jesus, is a spiritual one that cuts across political boundaries but does not deny political authority.

Revelations—Though the last book of the Bible contains many revelations, its proper name is singular—Revelation. The full title of the book is *The Revelation to John*, also known as *The Apocalypse.*

"Rose of Sharon"—The rose of Sharon referred to in Song of Solomon (2:1) is not the kind of flower called a rose today.

158

The plain of Sharon, the coastal lowland south of Lebanon, is known today for its annual profusion of wildflowers. The flower mentioned in the Song of Solomon seems to have been a bulbed plant. Scholars have suggested a type of crocus, perhaps the meadow saffron.

S

Sabbath vs. Sunday—Though Christians have long identified Sunday, the Lord's Day, with the Sabbath, the two holy days are distinct in the Bible.

Sabbath, which means "cessation," is used in the Bible to describe a sacred period of time when the faithful rest from their labors. It is most often identified with the seventh day of each week, from sundown Friday to sundown Saturday. Originally, the Sabbath was a time for everyone, even servants and animals, to rest and be refreshed (Ex 23:12; Dt 5:14). The weekly Sabbath was seen as a day to commune with God and to rest as he had rested after six days of creation (Gn 2:2, 3).

By Jesus' time, the character of the Sabbath observance had changed greatly. To the Pharisees, the Sabbath represented a day to please God through self-denial rather than a day that God had set aside for spiritual and physical renewal. The Sabbath observance had become encumbered with a complex and arduous set of prohibitions and restrictions which made the day a burden for the Jews rather than a blessing.

160

Jesus clashed with the Pharisees over the issue of Sabbath observance more than he did over any other single issue. All four Gospels record incidents in which the Pharisees criticized Jesus and his disciples for breaking the Sabbath; Jesus consistently responded that ceremonial law should be governed by compassion, neighborliness, or simple common sense. (*See* Mt 12:9–14; Mk 2:23–28; Lk 14:1–6: Jn 5:5–12.) Jesus did not seek to abolish the Sabbath, but to get back to the spirit of the Sabbath as originally instituted. All of his teachings about the Sabbath are summed up in his declaration: "The Sabbath was made for man, and not man for the Sabbath" (Mk 2:27).

According to the Gospels, Jesus arose from the dead on the first day of the week and appeared to his disciples again on the following Sunday. Very early in the life of the Christian church, Sunday became the Lord's Day, the day to worship him and to celebrate his resurrection (Acts 20:7, 1 Cor 16:2). Some Jewish Christians observed both the Sabbath and the Lord's Day (Acts 21:20), but the early Jerusalem Council did not include Sabbath obligations among the things expected of gentile Christians (Acts 15:29).

Sunday, also called "the Lord's Day" (Rv 1:10), soon absorbed many of the Sabbath associations as a day of rest set apart for worship and communion. Yet the apostle Paul warns several times that such observances should not become ends in themselves and that righteousness should not be equated with ritual obligation (Rom 14:5; Gal 4:9–10; Col 2:16).

Sailing and the sea—A Christian devotional booklet states that "Jonah took a cruise to Tarshish, instead of going to preach at Nineveh." A preacher suggests that

161

Jesus and his disciples sometimes went sailing on the Sea of Galilee to renew themselves and to escape the press of the crowds. But the Jews were not a maritime people, nor did they think of sailing as a form of leisure or relaxation. Rather they associated the sea with danger, hardship, and the forces of chaos arrayed against God.

The first chapter of the Bible reveals the Hebrew attitude toward the sea. Genesis 1:2 pictures the earth as formless, dark, and void with primordial waters not yet tamed by God's creative hand. In verses 6–10, God creates a firmament, or expanse, which divides the waters below from those above, thus making a dry place for animals and humans to inhabit. After creation, it is only God's sustaining hand that keeps the waters from overwhelming his creatures.

At the time of the flood, God removed this restraining influence and the waters submerged the entire earth. The flood was caused not simply by prolonged rain, but also by the breaking up of "the fountains of the deep" and the opening of "the windows of heaven" (Gn 7:11). Here again, as before creation, the seas are associated with a murky chaos.

Though water in the form of rain usually connotes blessing in the Bible, water in the form of the seas usually connotes hardship or danger. Besides Noah's flood, the Bible depicts Jonah, who escapes drowning only by God's provision of the "great fish"; Paul, who is shipwrecked three times (2 Cor 11:25); and Jesus' disciples, who are saved from a violent squall on the Sea of Galilee by his command to the wind and waves. (*See* 1 Kgs 22:27; Ps 24:4; and Jon 2:3–5.)

This theme, which appears so early in the Bible, carries through to the very end. Those who think of sailing as "almost heaven" will be disappointed to learn that in the Book of Revelation John envisions the new heaven and the new earth with no more oceans, no more watery chaos, to threaten God's people (Rv 21:1).

Saints—In the New Testament the word *saints* applies to all believers, not just to those who are exceptionally holy or those canonized by the church.

Saints in the New Testament are those who are sanctified, or consecrated, by their faith in Christ's redemption, not by singular or miraculous works of piety. Only in later church practice were individuals singled out as saints. (*See* Rom 16:15, 2 Cor 1:1, Phil 4:21).

Salome—The young woman who danced before Herod and demanded the head of John the Baptist is traditionally known as Salome, but she is never so identified in Scripture.

Three of the Gospels recount the death of John the Baptist (Mt 14:1–12, Mk 6:14–29, Lk 9:7–9). John had denounced Herod (the tetrarch, son of Herod the Great) for taking Herodias as his wife even though she was already married to his brother Philip. Herod imprisoned John but was reluctant to execute him because of his popularity. However, when Herodias's daughter danced before Herod on his birthday, she pleased him greatly, and he vowed to give her whatever she asked. At her mother's instruction, she asked for the head of John the Baptist on a platter.

The name of Herodias's daughter is not mentioned in any of the Gospel accounts. Josephus, the first-century Jewish historian, calls her Salome and that name has been adopted by tradition. Josephus also notes that Herod met humiliating defeat at the hands of his

163

Samson and Delilah; Gerrit van Honthorst; Cleveland Museum of Art; Mr. and Mrs. William H. Marlatt Fund.

brother Philip, a loss interpreted by many of his contemporaries as judgment for his capricious beheading of John the Baptist.

Samson and Delilah—Delilah is often pictured shearing off Samson's hair, the source of his strength, as he sleeps peacefully in her lap. Some pictures show Delilah using scissors to perform this unkindest cut of all, but scissors were unknown in ancient Israel.

Other illustrators show Delilah using a more plausible implement, a razor or knife. But this representation is still inaccurate, since Delilah didn't do the deed herself. She called in a man to shave off Samson's locks as he slept (Jgs 16:19).

Samson, Source of strength—Bible interpreters customarily note that Samson's strength was not inherent in his long, luxuriant hair. Rather, he was a Nazirite from birth, one specially devoted to God according to a sacred vow.

The Nazirites were individuals who set themselves apart for God, refusing to drink wine (which was associated with the heathen Canaanites), avoiding contact with the dead, and leaving their heads unshaven (Nm 6:1–6; Jgs 13:7). The cutting of Samson's hair, according to many interpreters, meant the breaking of his vow. Thus Samson's strength was broken when his oath was broken.

This approach has much to recommend it. Samson was set apart as a Nazirite even before his birth (Jgs 13:4–5). Also, Samson told Delilah, after much pleading on her part, that his strength derived from his Nazirite vow, one provision of which stated that his hair and beard should never be shaven (Jgs 16:17).

But this cannot be the whole reason Samson's strength is associated with his hair. Samson does not seem to have been very strict about observing his vows. He feasted for seven days at his first wedding (Jgs 14:10–12). The Hebrew word used to describe his feasting strongly suggests drinking as well as eating. Of course, Samson had more than a little contact with the dead, killing thirty Philistines on one occasion and 1,000 on another (Jgs 14:19, 15:15). Therefore, he had broken his vow before he ever met Delilah.

Samson was indiscreet in telling Delilah about the source of his strength, but his hair was cut by her treachery, not by his own will. Finally, the narrative in Judges 16 associates the return of Samson's strength with the growing back of his hair, apart from any mention of the Nazirite vow.

Saul becoming Paul—The apostle Paul is called both

165

The Conversion of Saint Paul; Jacopo Tintoretto; National Gallery of Art, Washington; Samuel H. Kress Collection.

Saul and Paul in the Book of Acts. Many readers assume that the two names represent a preconversion name (Saul) and a postconversion name (Paul), since Simon received a new name, Peter, from Jesus. But the name change does not coincide with Paul's conversion.

The apostle's name change is so firmly linked with his dramatic experience on the road to Damascus (Acts 9:1–19) that one annotated Bible (Scofield) begins referring to Saul as Paul in its headnotes five chapters before the new name ever appears in the actual text. In Acts, chapters 1–12, the apostle is known as Saul, even after his conversion. But when he undertakes his first missionary journey among the gentiles, he is referred to as "Saul (who also is called Paul)" (Acts 13:9). Thereafter he is known as Paul.

Saul and *Paul* are two different forms of the same name, Hebrew and Roman, respectively. The simplest explanation for the name change in Acts is that Saul,

166

the Jew, took the Roman form of his name once his ministry was predominantly among the Gentiles.

Scapegoat—In modern usage, a scapegoat is one who must bear the blame for an entire group to which he belongs even if he is innocent (or no more guilty than the others). In the Mosaic ritual, a scapegoat symbolically carried the sins of the people. But he was not sacrificed or harmed in any way. Instead he was let loose in the wilderness, a more fortunate fate than other animals who were not designated as scapegoats.

The scapegoat ritual is described in Leviticus 16:3–22. There Aaron, the high priest, was instructed to take two goats and cast lots over them. One was then sacrificed to the Lord as a sin offering, and the other, bearing the sins of the people, was taken into the wilderness and set free.

The word *scapegoat* in the KJV (v 8) is short for *escape goat*. The Hebrew word designating a goat as "scapegoat" is obscure. Some translations (such as the RSV) have taken it as a proper name, Azazel. In medieval Jewish tradition, Azazel was a hairy demon of the desert, whom the Israelites sought to appease. But no Azazel is mentioned anywhere else in Scripture, and it is out of keeping with Mosaic law for the Jews to make sacrifices to a demon or other rival to the Lord. Therefore, the King James translation, "scapegoat," is still considered valid.

Selah—The word *Selah*, found over seventy times in the Psalms, is not an Old Testament equivalent to *Amen*. The Hebrew word seems to suggest a pause, or cessation. It may be a liturgical note indicating a moment of silence or an instrumental interlude. But it is not spoken aloud as part of the psalm or said in confirmation of the words which precede it.

Sermon on the Mount—Jesus' lengthiest discourse (Mt 5–7) is never called the Sermon on the Mount in Scripture.

Matthew's Gospel reports that Jesus "went up into the mountain" to deliver the beatitudes and other teachings. A similar collection of teachings is recorded in the Gospel of Luke as being given on a level place, or plain (Lk 6:17).

One need not suppose that there is a contradiction between the two accounts. As an itinerant preacher and prophet, Jesus could have given the same discourse in a number of settings. Or Matthew may be referring generally to the mountainous region where the sermon was delivered, while Luke specifies a particular plateau or level spot among the hills.

Matthew may have emphasized the mountain setting of the sermon (or sermons) deliberately to portray Jesus as the new Moses bringing down divine teaching from a mountain. Note how Matthew's version of the discourse (but not Luke's) explicitly juxtaposes the teachings of Jesus with the law of Moses (5:21, 27, 31, 33, 38, 43).

Serpent in Eden—The Eden story seems to have generated more misconceptions than any other passage in the Bible. Apart from fallacies about the temptation (*See* APPLE, AS THE FORBIDDEN FRUIT) and the tempted (*See* SEX, AS THE FORBIDDEN FRUIT), there are two common assumptions about the tempter, the serpent, that deserve mention.

First, the tempting serpent has long been associated with Satan, but he is never so identified in the text (Gn 3). Some scholars argue that the serpent was assumed by the author to be an embodiment of Satan; others maintain that, when the Book of Genesis was written, the Hebrews did not yet have a clear concept of Satan as a full-fledged adversary of God.

Second, the serpent should not be imagined as a legless reptile crawling on its belly before the temptation; this is said to be a consequence of the Lord's curse (Gn 3:14).

Seventy times seven—In Jesus' teaching on forgiveness, the number "seventy times seven" is better rendered "seventy-seven times."

In Matthew 18:21–22, Peter asked Jesus if he should forgive a brother who sins against him as many as seven times. Jesus answered that he should forgive his brother "seventy times seven," according to the kjv. Though the Greek is ambiguous, a better reading would seem to be "seventy-seven times," as given in the jb and the marginal note of the rsv.

The meaning of this teaching, called the "law of forgiveness," is not changed by the number involved. Obviously, the point is that one shouldn't limit the number of times he or she forgives another. But the number seventy-seven offers a direct contrast to the law of vengeance in the Old Testament, where Lamech, a descendant of Cain, boasts that he will avenge himself on his enemies "seventy and sevenfold" (Gn 4:24).

Sex as the forbidden fruit—When people take the apple to be the forbidden fruit, they usually compound

169

their error by associating the apple with passion. They wrongly assume that "the knowledge of good and evil" is a euphemism for another kind of knowledge, carnal knowledge. The Fall, in the popular mind, is really about sex.

But Genesis makes clear that humans were created as sexual beings with the expectation that they would express their sexual natures. Before their sin, Adam and Eve were "naked and unashamed" (2:25), and they were given God's blessing to "be fruitful and multiply" (1:28). It was only after their disobedience that they realized their nakedness and sewed fig leaves to cover themselves (3:7). Only then did any sense of inhibition arise. The notion that the Fall resulted from illicit sexual activity comes from popular lore, not from the Book of Genesis.

Shadrach, Meshach, and Abednego—The three Israelites who walked around unharmed in Nebuchadnezzar's fiery furnace are popularly known by the names assigned to them by their conquerors, not by their true names.

Captive in Babylon with Daniel were his companions Hanaiah, Mishael, and Azariah. All four were given Babylonian names by their captors; Daniel was called Belteshazzar, and the others were called Shadrach, Meshach, and Abednego. Daniel continues to be called by his Hebrew name throughout the Book of Daniel, while the others are referred to by their Babylonian names. Since these three risked almost certain death to be true to the God of their fathers (Dn 3), it would seem more fitting, and more consistent with the retention of Daniel's name, that they be remembered as Hanaiah, Mishael, and Azariah.

"Spare the rod and spoil the child"—This proverb does not come from the Bible, but from *Hudibras*, a seventeenth-century satire by Samuel Butler. There is a similar saying, though, in the Book of Proverbs: "He that spareth his rod hateth his son: but he that loveth him chasteneth him betimes [promptly]" (Prv 13:24).

Star names in the Bible—English translations of the Old Testament generally call stars and constellations by the names we are familiar with today, not by their Hebrew names. This has given some readers the false impression that the Hebrews knew the constellations by the same names used by their Greek contemporaries—and that they must have known the Greek mythological figures after whom these constellations were named.

But the Hebrews had their own names for heavenly bodies. Consequently, translators must sometimes resort to guesswork to correlate Hebrew star names with those familiar to us today. For example, when the Lord speaks to Job out of the whirlwind, he asks if his questioners can command the stars with the same authority that their Creator does: "Can you bind the cluster of the Pleiades? or loose Orion's belt? Can you bring out the signs of the zodiac in their season? or guide Aldebaran and its train?" (Jb 38:31–32, NEB).

Translators agree on the first two constellations mentioned. The Hebrew name for the Pleiades seems to mean "the Cluster," imagined perhaps as a string of gold beads. Orion, the Hunter, is in Hebrew "The Burly One." On the next two lines, though, there is wide divergence. The phrase *signs of the zodiac* is a highly speculative rendering of a single Hebrew word,

171

mazzaroth. The JB identifies this as "the morning star," while other translations simply call it a "constellation" (NASB) or retain the Hebrew name, *mazzaroth* (KJV, RSV). Likewise, the name identified above as *Aldebaran* is alternatively identified as "Arcturus" (KJV) and the "Bear" (JB, RSV, NASB). These differing translations are light years apart.

Lest the original point get lost amid these speculations, the Hebrews had their own names for the stars and constellations and would not have been familiar with the Greek, Roman, and Arabic names by which these are known to us today.

Straight is the gate—The gateway to life, according to Jesus, is not "straight," as opposed to crooked, but "strait" (narrow) as opposed to wide.

In Matthew 7:13–14, Jesus contrasted the gate taken by the many with the gate taken by the few:

> Enter ye in at the strait gate: for wide is the gate, and broad is the way, that leadeth to destruction, and many there be which go in thereat: Because strait is the gate, and narrow is the way, which leadeth unto life, and few there be that find it.

Strait is an archaic word meaning "narrow" or "tight." It survives mainly in the phrases "strait jacket" and "dire straits" as well as in the term for a narrow waterway (e.g., Strait of Magellan). The word has been altered to "straight" in the phrase "walking the straight and narrow," but there is no reference to straightness, or crookedness, in this parable of Jesus.

Subdue the earth—When the Lord tells Adam and Eve

in Genesis 1 to multiply, replenish the earth, and subdue it, his instructions have alarmed some ecology-
minded readers. This blessing seems to encourage
exploitation of the natural environment without regard to long-term consequences. Bible expositors have
tried to affirm the ecological sensitivity of Scripture
by explaining that the word *subdue* in Genesis means
simply "be good stewards of." But this interpretation is
not supported by the Hebrew.

The word in question is found in Genesis 1:28, where
God blesses Adam and Eve after having created them
in his own image: "Be fruitful, and multiply, and replenish the earth and subdue it: and have dominion
over the fish of the sea, and over the fowl of the air, and
over every living thing that moveth upon the earth."
The phrase "have dominion" in this verse creates no
problem for ecologists since humans can exercise dominion over their natural environment without de-
stroying it. But the word "subdue," according to some
cultural historians, has encouraged the attitude that
nature has no value or purpose apart from the ways it
can be exploited for human ends.

The Hebrew word translated "subdue" in this verse
cannot be softened to "be good stewards of." In fact, the
sense of the Hebrew is even harsher than the English
word *subdue*. Hebrew *kabash* means literally "to tread
down, to conquer." The word is used elsewhere in the
Old Testament to refer to conquest of land (Nm 32:22),
subjection of slaves (Neh 5:5), and treading others under one's feet (Zec 9:15). (*Kabash* is also the likeliest
source of the Yiddish phrase "put the kibosh on"—that
is, to put an end to something.)

Of course, there was no ecological issue in biblical
times, since the powers of nature were much more

likely to subdue humans than humans were likely to subdue nature. Also, God's instruction to subdue the earth was given to Adam and Eve in their unfallen state; such a broad mandate was not offered again after the Fall. When humanity started over again after the flood, Noah and his family were again blessed along with all the creatures they carried with them in the ark. They were instructed to "be fruitful and multiply, and replenish the earth" (Gn 9:1). Notice that this time there is no mention of subduing the earth.

Subjection of wives—The Bible does not teach that women in general should be subservient to men in general, but it does teach that wives should be "in subjection" to their husbands. Some interpreters, who see an egalitarian model of marriage in the New Testament, argue that while subjection involves voluntary service, it does not accord any authority to the husband which is not shared by the wife. However, the Greek word translated "subjection" does not suggest the idea of self-imposed servanthood.

The teaching about the subjection of wives comes in 1 Peter 3:1: "Likewise, ye wives, be in subjection to your husbands; that, if any obey not the word, they may also be won by the conversation of the wives." Some commentators emphasize the second phrase in this verse about conversation and mutual communication, but that qualifying statement does not negate the preceding admonitions about subjection and obedience. The Greek word used for "subjection" plainly denotes submission to authority or greater power. The same Greek word occurs in the New Testament to describe the subjection of demons to the disciples' power (Lk 10:17), subjection of children to their parents

174

(1 Tm 3:4), and the subjection of slaves to their masters (1 Pt 2:18). Obviously, none of these involves mutual authority or self-imposed servanthood.

Of course, a well-rounded understanding of the Bible's teaching on marriage cannot be derived from one verse. (*See* Eph 5:21–33). Neither should we distort the meaning of a particular verse to make it conform to our prior assumptions.

"Suffer the children"—A recent television documentary on world hunger was titled *Suffer the Children,* as was an article on child abuse in a popular magazine. But Jesus' words "Suffer the children" do not refer to the pain or privation of children.

The context of Jesus' words makes their meaning clear (Mk 10:13–16; Mt 19:13–15; Lk 18:15–17). When the multitudes flocked after Jesus in Judea, many parents brought with them children to be blessed. Jesus' disciples began to scold and turn away those who had brought children, but Jesus became indignant, and corrected them: "Suffer the little children to come unto me, and forbid them not: for of such is the kingdom of heaven" (Mk 10:14).

In this context, the word *suffer* means "allow" or "do not hinder." (Similarly, "women's suffrage" means that women should be allowed to vote.) Because of confusion over this word in the KJV, modern English translations render Jesus' words as "Permit the children to come to me," or "Let the children come."

Sweating blood in Gethsemane—Some paintings of Jesus praying on the night before his crucifixion portray him with red drops running down his forehead as if he were already wearing the crown of thorns. But

175

Luke's Gospel says that "his sweat was as it were great drops of blood falling down to the ground" (22:44b). That is, Jesus, in his agony, sweat profusely as if he were bleeding, but he did not sweat blood.

Swords into plowshares—Isaiah 2:4 predicts a time of universal peace under the Lord's rulership:

> And he shall judge among the nations, and shall rebuke many people: and they shall beat their swords into plowshares, and their spears into pruninghooks: nation shall not lift up sword against nation, neither shall they learn war anymore.

Though the word *ploughshares* in the KJV is retained in most modern English translations, it is an anachronism. "Ploughshare" is not simply an archaic word for *plow*. It is the cutting blade of a moldboard plow, a kind of plow developed in Europe during the early Middle Ages to cut and turn over heavy turf.

Though this verse is often quoted at peace rallies, the Bible does not teach that implements of peace are always more desirable than implements of war. The prophet Joel, for example, describes "the day of the Lord" not in terms of universal peace, but in terms of Israel's military victory over its enemies: "Beat your ploughshares into swords, and your pruning hooks into spears: let the weak say, I am strong" (Jl 3:10).

T

"Take no thought"—Jesus' repeated advice to his disciples to take no thought for the necessities of life is not a mandate to abandon all prudence and foresight.

In the KJV, Jesus advises his disciples to "take no thought" for their food, drink, or clothing (Mt 6:31); to "take no thought" for the morrow (6:34); to "take no thought" what to say if questioned by the authorities (10:19); and even to "take no thought" for their very lives (6:25). These verses have been quoted as evidence that Jesus was an impractical visionary whose ideas could not actually be put into common practice.

But the phrase "take no thought" in the KJV means, "Do not entertain fearful thoughts." In the verses mentioned above, all the modern English translations replace "take no thought" with "do not worry" or "do not be anxious."

Taking the Lord's name in vain—To most people, "taking the Lord's name in vain" is a "Bible language" term for swearing. However, the third commandment forbids more than just verbal disrespect for holy things.

For the Hebrews, like most of the ancients, a person

and his name were one. The most sacred of all names was the personal name of God, Yahweh, a name that Jews considered so wondrous and holy that they avoided writing it or uttering it aloud. To speak the name of God was to invoke his very person, since the name of the Lord *was* the Lord. To "take God's name in vain" was not simply to show disrespect. It was to profane the name of God by invoking the Lord's power or authority for unholy purposes. This could involve invoking a curse, uttering a false oath, or speaking the name as part of a magical rite or ceremony of divination.

Talents—Jesus' parable of the talents contrasts the two faithful servants who doubled the money entrusted to them with the indolent servant who buried his talent rather than investing it wisely (Mt 25:14–30). Readers of the parable may wonder what the master expected his servant to do with a single talent (v 15), since the amount does not seem to be large enough to do anything but hide it for safe-keeping.

In reality, a talent was not a single coin. It was a great sum of money—sixty coins of gold or silver, a lifetime's worth of wages for commoners. The timid servant feared to invest the money not because it was so little, but because it was so great an amount.

Sermons on the parable of the talents customarily end with an exhortation not to hide one's talent as the unwise servant did. Whether or not a pun is intended, the modern word *talent*, signifying a special gift or ability, does indeed come from this parable.

Teetotalism as biblical teaching—The Bible con-

178

demns drunkenness, but it does not altogether forbid consumption of alcohol. Those who say that the Bible advocates temperance should realize that *temperance* does not mean abstinence, but rather temperate, or moderate, drinking.

Both the Old Testament and New Testament contain explicit admonitions against drunkenness (Is 5:11, 22; Prv 23:20–21; Rom 13:13, Gal 5:21). But wine and strong drink are also mentioned in connection with celebration and festivity without disapproval (Gn 43:34, Ps 104:15, Am 9:13, Jn 2:1–11). In biblical times the common people drank a diluted form of wine as their table beverage and saved the better wines for special occasions (*See* Jn 2:1–11).

Those who took a Nazirite vow might abstain from wine and strong drink for a time and from cutting their hair. But there were no actual teetotalers in the Bible, ones who considered alcoholic consumption inherently objectionable. (Incidentally, the *tee* in *teetotaler* is meant to emphasize *total* abstinence from alcohol. It should not be spelled "teatotaler" as if the drinker has switched from alcohol to caffeine.) (*See also* WINE AS NONALCOHOLIC.)

Tent of meeting—As the Israelites wandered through the wilderness, they carried a portable tent-shrine called the tent of meeting. Many readers have assumed from the name that the tent of meeting was for the purposes of general assembly, a cloth meeting-hall in which all the people gathered on special occasions. But the tent of meeting was a place for Moses to meet with God, not a place for mass assembly.

The best description of the tent of meeting is in Exodus 33:7–11. There it is explained that the tent of

179

meeting was pitched far outside the camp for those who wanted to seek the Lord's presence. According to this chapter, Moses went out to the tent for special face-to-face encounters with the Lord to receive specific oracles and instructions (vv 9, 11). Though the tent of meeting was sometimes used as a place where Jewish leaders could gather together before the Lord (Nm 11:16, 17; 12:1–8), its designation as a tent of meeting referred primarily to its function as a place for God to meet his people.

"Thou shalt not kill"—In debates concerning pacifism or the death penalty, someone inevitably quotes the sixth commandment: "Thou shalt not kill" (Ex 20:13; Dt 5:17). But this commandment is not a sweeping order to avoid taking human life under any circumstance.

Even a cursory look at the Old Testament reveals situations in which killing was condoned or even commanded. In war the Israelites were sometimes told to destroy not only the soldiers of their enemies, but also the women and children (Dt 20:16, 17). And the Book of Exodus, where the words "thou shalt not kill" are found, recommends the death penalty not only for murder (21:12), but also for witchcraft (22:18), bestiality (22:19), worshiping other gods (22:20), and cursing one's parents (21:17).

The Hebrew word used in the sixth commandment refers in this context to the unlawful taking of life. That is why some modern English translations (NEB, JB) render the sixth commandment as "You shall not murder."

Three Kings—The traditional Christmas carol about

The Adoration of the Magi; Botticelli; National Gallery of Art, Washington; Andrew W. Mellon Collection.

the wise men visiting Bethlehem begins "We three kings of Orient are." This line is biblically accurate except that there were not necessarily three who came, they weren't kings, and they weren't from the Orient, as the term is used today.

Matthew, chapter 2, states that "wise men" came from the east seeking the King of the Jews, but it does not specify their number (v 1). The wise men brought three gifts with them—gold, frankincense, and myrrh (v 11). Tradition has pictured three wise men with one gift each, but there is no statement in the text to that effect.

The "wise men" were not kings in the sense of political rulers, but magi, court advisors or perhaps astrologers. Matthew's account says that the magi saw a "star in the east" before coming to Jerusalem, but it does not say that the star guided them until after they had seen

181

Ancient bronze mirror with sculptured handle from Egypt, of the type that Israelite women took with them on the Exodus. The Metropolitan Museum of Art; Gift of Miss Helen Miller Gould, 1910.

Herod and then journeyed south toward Bethlehem (vv 2, 9).

Christmas creches usually depict the wise men kneeling before Jesus in the manger. But verse 11 says that the baby Jesus was in a house by the time the magi arrived from the east. "The east," in this context, means east of Palestine. The word *Orient* in the carol simply means east, not the Far East.

"Through a glass darkly"—When the apostle Paul wrote about seeing "through a glass darkly," he was not referring to a smoky or opaque pane of glass. He was thinking of a looking glass, a mirror.

Paul writes to the church at Corinth, "For now we see through a glass darkly; but then face to face: now I

182

know in part; but then shall I know even as also I am known" (1 Cor 13:12). In this verse Paul is contrasting a dim reflection in a mirror with face-to-face reality. Mirrors in ancient times were made of polished metal; therefore the images they reflected were considerably less distinct than those of modern-day mirrors.

The Greek word translated "glass" in this passage is *esoptron*, literally "something to look into." It is the same word for mirror used in James 1:23–24: "For if any be a hearer of the word, and not a doer, he is like unto a man beholding his natural face in a glass: For he beholdeth himself, and goeth his way, and straightway forgetteth what manner of man he was."

"Tongues, they will cease"—Those who oppose speaking in tongues in contemporary Christian worship argue that glossalalia, or ecstatic utterance, may have been appropriate in the New Testament church, but it is not meant for modern Christians. Some opponents of speaking in tongues quote Paul's prediction in 1 Corinthians that tongues will cease. The context of the quotation, however, indicates that this verse should not be applied to the current debate about the use of tongues.

The phrase comes from 1 Corinthians, chapter 13, the famous discourse on love. In verses 8–10, Paul contrasts the eternal nature of love with the temporal nature of other aspects of the Christian life:

> Love never ends; as for prophecies, they will pass away; as for tongues, they will cease; as for knowledge, it will pass away. For our knowledge is imperfect and our prophecy is imperfect; but when the perfect comes, the imperfect will pass away (1 Cor 13:8–10, RSV).

183

In this passage tongues are offered as an example of finite things, along with prophecy and knowledge. Though many people would say that prophecy has ceased, none would argue that knowledge has ceased in the modern age. Also, Paul implies that these things will not cease until the perfect comes, most likely referring to the return of Christ. In context, then, Paul's statement that tongues will cease has little relevance to discussions about the appropriateness of tongues in Christian worship today.

"To whom shall we go?"—A recent advertisement for a Christian missionary organization featured as its headline Peter's question to Jesus: "To whom shall we go?" Without explanation the reader is left to assume that Peter was eager to share the gospel and that he simply wanted to know where to begin. The context, though, reveals a very different situation.

Peter's question was not about those who remained to be evangelized. Rather Peter was telling Jesus that he was the only one the disciples could turn to. Many of Jesus' early followers left him after hearing his difficult teaching on partaking of his flesh (Jn 6:66). When Jesus asked his chosen disciples if they too would abandon him, Peter answered, "To whom shall we go? thou hast the words of eternal life. And we believe and are sure that thou art the Christ, the Son of the living God" (Jn 6:68–69).

Tree of Life as forbidden fruit—The forbidden fruit eaten by Adam and Eve was not taken from the tree of life, and their sin was not simply a desire for immortality.

184

The Temptation of Christ;
Juan de Flandes; National
Gallery of Art, Washington;
Ailsa Mellon Bruce Fund.

Of all the trees in the garden, only one was forbidden: "And the Lord God commanded the man, saying, "You may freely eat of every tree of the garden; but of the tree of the knowledge of good and evil you shall not eat, for in the day that you eat of it you shall die" (2:17, RSV).

This, of course, is the very tree from which they did eat because they wanted to be "like God, knowing good and evil" (3:5). Their sin was not a desire for immortality; the tree of life was not forbidden to them until after their disobedience. Their sin was the disobedience itself and the presumption that they might become equals with their Creator.

Turning stones to bread—Songs and sermons about world hunger have recommended that, like God, we

185

should turn stones to bread for those who are starving. This occurs nowhere in the Bible, however. The idea of turning stones to bread does appear in the Bible, but it is the devil's suggestion.

During his forty days of fasting in the wilderness, Jesus was tempted by Satan to relieve his hunger by miraculously changing the stones into bread (Mt 4:3). Jesus' reply is much better known than the original temptation: "It is written, Man shall not live by bread alone, but by every word that proceedeth out of the mouth of God" (v 4).

U

"**Unequally yoked**"—In his second letter to the church at Corinth, Paul encouraged his readers to avoid becoming unequally yoked. This exhortation has been taken by some readers as a teaching against interracial marriage. However, the passage makes no reference either to race or to marriage.

In 2 Corinthians 6:14–15, Paul warns the Christians at Corinth about becoming too involved with unbelievers:

> Be ye not unequally yoked together with unbelievers: for what fellowship hath righteousness with unrighteousness? and what communion hath light with darkness? And what concord hath Christ with Belial? or what part hath he that believeth with an infidel?

It is clear from the context that the apostle is referring to believers mixing with unbelievers in all areas of life, not just marriage relationships. It is equally clear from all the parallel questions that "light" and "darkness" refer to spiritual illumination or its absence, not to skin color. (*See also* DIVIDING LIGHT AND DARK; *for a discussion of Belial see* MAMMON.)

V

"Vanity of vanities"—This recurring phrase in the Book of Ecclesiastes does not refer to excessive pride or self-love. It is, rather, a comment on the emptiness and futility of life for those without any transcendent frame of reference.

The phrase "vanity of vanities . . . all is vanity" appears near the beginning of Ecclesiastes (1:2) and again near the end (12:8). In between these somber pronouncements, the author surveys the meaningless cycle of life (1:4–11) and notes the final emptiness of wisdom (1:12–18), of pleasure and money (2:1–11), and of hard work (2:18–23). These pessimistic and sometimes paradoxical musings continue throughout the book until the last two verses. There the lengthy diagnosis of the vanity of life is followed by a terse prescription: "Let us hear the conclusion of the whole matter: Fear God, and keep his commandments: for this is the whole duty of man. For God shall bring every work unto judgment, with every secret thing, whether it be good or whether it be evil" (12:13–14).

"Vengeance is mine, saith the Lord"—This phrase

188

from the apostle Paul means the opposite of what most people think. Paul's words do not provide an excuse for taking vengeance in the Lord's name. Rather, they assert that vengeance is the Lord's task, *not* to be carried out by humans.

In Romans 12:19–21, Paul counsels against human reprisals:

> Dearly beloved, avenge not yourselves, but rather give place unto wrath: for it is written, Vengeance is mine, I will repay, saith the Lord. Therefore if thine enemy hunger, feed him; if he thirst, give him drink: for in so doing thou shalt heap coals of fire on his head. Be not overcome of evil, but overcome evil with good.

Here Paul urges his readers to practice kindness and to let God take care of vengeance. The metaphor of heaping coals on one's enemy comes from Proverbs 25:21–22. In ancient times defenders of a walled city would pour hot coals on the heads of their enemies climbing up the siege ladders. The proverb quoted by Paul suggests that one can best take revenge upon enemies by "killing them with kindness."

Vinegar given to Jesus on the cross—When Jesus cried, "I thirst" from the cross, he was offered a sponge soaked in vinegar (Jn 19:28–30). Many readers, knowing the sourness of vinegar, have assumed that this was just one more way in which Jesus' tormentors mocked him, along with their jeering and spitting and putting the crown of thorns on his head. However, the vinegar was probably offered as a painkiller, not as a bitter drink given to a desperately thirsty man.

The word *vinegar* means "sour wine." Though vinegar is now commonly used as a condiment and preservative, some forms of vinegar can also be used as a beverage. The word translated vinegar in the KJV and the RSV is called "wine" or "sour wine" in other English versions (NASB, NEB, JB). This may have been the cheap wine drunk by the Roman soldiers.

Mark 15:23 reports that Jesus was also offered "wine mingled with myrrh." This was almost certainly a painkiller, but Jesus refused to drink it. Perhaps he wanted to avoid its drugging effects. The vinegar offered him just before his death, then, need not seen as one more heartless torment; it may well have represented an act of compassion by one of those watching the crucifixion.

Vision of the dry bones—Many people who hear the words, usually in parody, "the hipbone's connected to the thighbone" have no idea what the words refer to. These words come from a black spiritual based on the prophet Ezekiel's vision of the dry bones coming back to life. The song apparently takes Ezekiel's vision as a promise of bodily resurrection for believers. But Ezekiel's vision refers instead to the restoration of the shattered nation of Israel.

In Ezekiel 37:1–10, the prophet sees a valley full of dried bones. The Lord instructs Ezekiel to prophesy that the bones will be regathered and that they will take on flesh and sinews. Ezekiel speaks the prophecy with the result that the bones begin to rattle, to come together, and to reclothe themselves in flesh and skin. Then Ezekiel prophesies again at the Lord's bidding until the four winds blow over the newly made bodies.

The breath of the Lord enters into them and causes the remains of all those slain to rise up and live again.

It is easy to see how this vision can be taken as a promise of bodily resurrection. And it could be argued that, from a New Testament perspective, Ezekiel's vision would find a richer fulfillment than even the one the prophet foresaw. In context, though, Ezekiel is not predicting the bodily resurrection of particular individuals, but rather the restoration of the nation Israel.

Vocation as a "calling"—The word *vocation* comes from the Latin word *vocatio*, "calling." Especially among Protestants, one hears the idea that God calls individuals to specific trades or occupations. The Bible speaks of discipleship as a "calling," but it does not specifically teach that occupational choices are ordained by God.

The idea that God chooses specific occupations for believers comes mainly from the leaders of the Reformation. Emphasizing the sovereignty of God in all areas of life, Martin Luther and John Calvin expanded the biblical concept of the "calling" to include not only the call to salvation but also the other major decisions of one's life. The Puritans, as part of their well-known work ethic, adopted the idea that a believer's trade or occupation was a sacred trust. They felt that some members of the elect were called to be ordained ministers and that others were called just as fully to be ordained farmers or tradesmen.

The words *calling* and *vocation* in the Bible, though, are not defined so broadly. In Scripture, a calling is an invitation by God to salvation and to special service. In the Old Testament, patriarchs and prophets are chosen by God to speak and act in his name (Gn 12:2; Ex 3:4;

191

Jer 1:4–9). In the New Testament, the "calling" denotes an invitation to be saved and a communal responsibility to live according to that call (Eph 4:1–4; 2 Tm 1:9). The Bible does not teach, however, that God designates particular professions for those who respond to his call.

W

"Where there is no vision, the people perish"—This phrase, surely one of the most memorable and quotable in the KJV, may also be one of the most misleading.

Proverbs 29:18, in the KJV reads: "Where there is no vision, the people perish: but he that keepeth the law, happy is he." The first phrase is usually taken to mean that a society cannot survive without a coherent sense of meaning and value shared by its members. But the Hebrew word translated "vision" is more specific than this and the Hebrew translated "perish" is more general.

The word *vision* in the Hebrew means the oracle or revelation given to a prophet, that which he communicates to the people as the will of the Lord. The word rendered "perish" in the KJV means generally "loosen," which can be interpreted various ways in various contexts. Elsewhere in the KJV the word is translated "expose," "dismiss," "go back," "refuse," and "uncover," but nowhere else is it interpreted as "perish."

Modern translations generally choose variations of the word *loosen* which preserve the contrast between the first part of the proverb and the second part about

193

keeping the law. The RSV declares, "Where there is no prophecy, the people cast off restraint," and the JB says, "Where there is no vision, the people get out of hand." Though these translations do not exactly etch themselves into the memory, they reflect more accurately the sense of the original Hebrew.

"Where two or three are gathered"—Jesus said, "Where two or three are gathered together in my name, there am I in the midst of them" (Mt 18:20). This promise is usually taken to mean that two or three believers together constitute a kind of spiritual quorum—that the Spirit of Christ is present in a group of two or three in a way he is not present for individual believers. But the context of Jesus' words reveals a different emphasis.

Jesus' promise came at the conclusion of a teaching about church discipline: how to deal with a brother who has given offense (Mt 18:15–19). Jesus recommended that first someone should confront the offender one-on-one about his misconduct. If he refuses to listen, one should take one or two others along, so that "two or three witnesses" can agree together about what is said. If the offender still refuses to face the issue, then he must be confronted by the church as a whole.

Jesus seemed to have in mind the Mosaic law that a person cannot be convicted of a serious offense unless there are at least two or three witnesses (Dt 17:6, 19:15). When Jesus promised to be where "two or three are gathered," he was speaking not about the quorum for a prayer meeting, but about the number needed to confirm a church member's misconduct. Jesus assured his followers that where a sufficient number agree,

194

their judgment will be confirmed in heaven (vv 18–19; see also 1 Tm 5:19, Heb 10:28).

"Where you go, I will go"—In the Book of Ruth are found these beautiful words of loyalty and devotion: "For where you go I will go, and where you lodge I will lodge; your people shall be my people, and your God my God" (1:16, RSV). Since these words have often been quoted in marriage ceremonies and on engagement announcements, many people assume that the words were originally spoken to a husband or lover. But with these words Ruth's vow expressed her loyalty to her mother-in-law, Naomi.

Because of a famine in their homeland of Judah, Naomi had traveled with her husband and two sons to the neighboring country of Moab. The two sons married Moabite women, one of whom was Ruth. In time, though, the husband and two sons died, leaving all three women as widows. Naomi decided to return to her home country and encouraged her widowed daughters-in-law to go back to their own people to find husbands. But Ruth clung to Naomi and uttered the well-known words quoted above. The rest of the Book of Ruth tells how she returned with Naomi and found in Judah a most suitable husband, Boaz.

"Wickedness in high places"—More than one critic of Big Government or Big Business has quoted the biblical phrase "wickedness in high places" when referring to those who use power or influence for unjust ends. But the apostle Paul's warning to the Christians at Ephesus is about superhuman powers, not about highly placed human rulers.

195

In his Epistle to the Ephesians, Paul warns that the spiritual battle is not like earthly combat:

> Put on the whole armor of God, that ye may be able to stand against the wiles of the devil. For we wrestle not against flesh and blood, but against principalities, against powers, against the rulers of the darkness of this world, against spiritual wickedness in high places (Eph 6:11–12).

In the Greek, "high places" refers to literal height—the heavens. The evil powers mentioned by Paul are spiritual (that is, nonphysical) forces outside the earthly realm.

Widow's mite—What is called the "widow's mite" is, in the Gospel accounts, actually two mites, still a paltry sum.

The story of the "widow's mite" comes from Jesus' last appearance in the temple of Jerusalem (Mk 12:41–44; Lk 21:1–4). Jesus saw rich men casting their gifts into the treasury, followed by an impoverished widow who put in two mites, two copper coins worth less than a penny. Jesus regarded her gift as greater than those of the rich men since she had given all she had.

Wine as nonalcoholic grape juice—The notion that the wine mentioned in the New Testament was actually a nonalcoholic grape drink is hard to swallow.

The wine mentioned in the New Testament is clearly an alcoholic beverage. John the Baptist drank "neither wine nor strong drink" (Lk 1:15). The apostles, newly filled with the Holy Spirit, were accused of being "full of new wine" (Acts 2:13), but Peter answered that men do not get drunk so early in the day (v 15). In his epistles, Paul frequently exhorts his readers not to be drunk with wine. This admonition would not make sense if wine were only a kind of grape juice.

In a hot climate like Palestine, an unfermented grape drink would quickly spoil and, therefore, would not be practical as a beverage. The wine of the New Testament is unquestionably alcoholic, though the common people probably drank a more diluted form than most of the wines available today.

Wisdom of Solomon—The wisdom of Solomon is proverbial. Yet the historical accounts in the Bible do not always present him as a discerning or faithful ruler.

The Bible speaks a great deal about the wisdom of Solomon. The First Book of Kings says that he composed 3,000 proverbs and 1,500 songs (4:32). It also explains that when the Lord offered to give him whatever he wanted, Solomon did not ask for riches or long life, but for an "understanding heart" to rule his people. The Lord was so pleased with Solomon's request that he granted him wisdom, as well as wealth and longevity (3:5–12). The wisdom of Solomon and the splendor of his court so amazed the Queen of Sheba that she was literally breathless (1 Kgs 10:1–6).

Yet this splendor had its price. Solomon inherited a strong, prosperous kingdom from his father David and he left it in such a weakened condition that it collapsed soon after his death. The building of Solomon's lavish palace and temple required the use of forced labor (1 Kgs 5:13), and it drew heavily from the resources of the kingdom. Of all Israel's kings, Solomon's reign best illustrated the prophets' perennial complaints about

197

the extravagance of the privileged minority amid the grievous poverty of the majority.

According to First Kings, Solomon also added many non-Jewish wives and concubines to his harem, thus disobeying the Lord's commands not to take "strange women" (11:1). He also built heathen temples for them and offered sacrifices even to the god Molech, an abomination to the Jews (11:7–8). For all the wisdom attributed to Solomon early in the accounts of his reign, the chronicle closes with the story of his apostasy that "Solomon did evil in the sight of the Lord, and went not fully after the Lord, as did David his father" (11:6).

Witch of Endor—The woman who conjured up the spirit of the dead Samuel for King Saul is usually called the witch of Endor. The word *witch* makes modern readers think of cauldron-stirring hags, the kind of women consulted by MacBeth. The woman of Endor is better designated a medium.

Saul went to the woman of Endor in desperation (1 Sm 28:1–25). His enemies the Philistines were massing on his borders, and they were joined by David and his fighting men. Saul sought the oracle of the Lord to find out what to do, but he received no answer since he had lost God's favor. Even though Saul had earlier rid his country of sorcerers and necromancers, he asked his servants to find someone with a "familiar spirit" for him to consult with. They told him, not about the witch of Endor, but about the woman who had a familiar spirit (1 Sm 28:7).

Saul went in disguise to see the medium, and she conjured up the spirit of the prophet Samuel, who had been Saul's trusted advisor. Samuel's apparition told Saul that the battle with the Philistines would be lost and that Saul would soon join Samuel in the realm of shadows.

The word *medium* has less unsavory connotations than *witch*. But the woman's practice of necromancy was a serious offense in ancient Israel, punishable by banishment or even death (Ex 22:18; Dt 18:10–11).

X

Xmas—Some Christians object to the abbreviation "XMAS" by saying that it "crosses out Christ." But "XMAS" is not a recent, secularized abbreviation.

The letter *X* stands for the Greek *chi* (also written *X*), the first letter of the word *Christ* in Greek. For centuries before the modern "XMAS," with its commercial connotations, scholars, both Christian and non-Christian, have been using the abbreviation *X* for *Christ* and *Xn* for *Christian*.

Y

"Your zeal hath provoked many"—When Paul writes to the Christians at Corinth, "Your zeal hath provoked many," he does not mean that others have been offended by their earnestness. Rather, he compliments them because others have been stirred to good works by their example.

The context in the KJV makes the apostle's meaning clear: "For I know the forwardness of your mind, for which I boast of you to them in Macedonia: . . . and your zeal hath provoked very many" (2 Cor 9:2). The word *provoke* in the KJV means "to arouse, stir up," without any negative connotations. Since the word now suggests anger or annoyance, modern English translations replace "provoked" with "stirred up" (RSV, NASB), or other less vexacious verbs.

"You say that I am"—According to Luke's Gospel, Jesus was brought before the Jewish assembly of elders for questioning on the morning after his arrest. When they asked him if he was the Son of God, he answered, "You say that I am." Many scholars feel that this answer was not an evasion; rather it was an idiomatic expression meaning, "Yes, I am."

In Luke, chapter 22, Jesus was brought before the chief priests and scribes, who asked him if he was the Christ. His reply and the ensuing confrontation are recounted in detail:

> If I tell you, you will not believe; and if I ask you, you will not answer. But from now on the Son of man shall be seated at the right hand of the power of God." And they all said, "Are you the Son of God, then?" And he said to them, "You say that I am." And they said, "What further testimony do we need? We have heard it ourselves from his own lips" (Lk 22:67–71, RSV).

Jesus' answer, "You say that I am," is not entirely clear, but it is not a simple evasion. The expression used here may well be an affirmation like the modern slang phrase, "You said it!" The response of the Jews present indicates that they took his answer to be a blasphemous assertion of his own deity, not an attempt to avoid answering.

Since the expression translated "You say that I am" is unfamiliar to modern readers, some contemporary English versions of the Bible offer more unambiguous wording. To the question "Are you the Son of God?" the NASB records Jesus' answer plainly as, "Yes, I am." The NEB gives the alternative reading, "You are right, for I am."

Z

Zealous God/Jealous God—Bible readers are often confused by descriptions of the Lord as a "jealous God." They wonder how a trait considered immature or unworthy in human beings should become sanctified and praiseworthy when found in God. The problem is compounded for those who discover that the words *jealous* and *zealous* are sometimes used interchangeably in the Bible to describe God's passion for his chosen people.

In English usage, the words *zealous* and *jealous* have contrasting meanings. In the noun forms, *zeal* generally connotes positive emotion, enthusiasm or commitment, while *jealousy* connotes negative emotion, envy or possessiveness. But the two words are derived ultimately from the same Greek word, *zelos*, "passion, ardor."

Like the Greek, the Hebrew language has one word for an emotional state which can be described positively or negatively, a passion *for* or a passion *against*. There is no exact English equivalent for this term, but it describes a vehement impulse to protect that which is rightfully due and a rage when that rightful due is denied. This zealous/jealous passion can be centered on one's own rightful due or on that of others.

In humans, this emotion can manifest itself as mere envy. The Hebrew word translated both "jealousy" and "zeal" is used in Genesis 26:14 to describe the Philistines' feelings about Isaac's prosperity, their resentment that he seems to have more than his share. The term is found again in Genesis 37:11 when Joseph's brothers covet the special favor he has found with their father.

But the same Hebrew term describes the zeal of the righteous to give God what is due him. Elijah says that he has been "jealous for the Lord" when so many others have turned to false gods (1 Kgs 19:14). The psalmist describes his consuming devotion by telling the Lord that "the zeal of thine house hath eaten me up" (Ps 69:9).

The Lord himself is described in the Bible as having the same fervor. He is a "jealous God" because he expects the worship and obedience due to him as the one true God (Ex 20:5, Dt 5:9). He is also *jealous* for his people and for Jerusalem (Zec 1:14) with a *zeal* to fulfill his promise in them (Is 9:7; 37:32).

Given this context, it should not seem paradoxical that God can be described (Jl 2:18) as *jealous* for his land in some English translations (KJV, RSV, NIV), and *zealous* for his land in others (NASB, NEB).

Endnotes

Absalom, Burnam (1975), p. 1.

Adam, children of. Burnam (1975), p. 48.

Almost persuaded. *Wycliffe*, p. 1173.

Ancient of Days. Hastings, p. 31.

Ararat. Hastings, p. 49; Smith, p. 47.

Ark of the Covenant as a weapon. Hastings, p. 53.

Arks in the Old Testament. Burnam (1980), pp. 8–9.

Balm in Gilead. Hastings, pp. 4, 85.

Barbarous people. *Wycliffe*, p. 1176.

B.C. and A.D. Finegan, pp. 132–33.

Birthdate of Jesus. Burnam (1975), pp. 49–50; Finegan, p. 233.

Blaspheming the Holy Spirit. *Harper*, p. 1499.

Bosom of Abraham. McKenzie, p. 6.

Burying one's father. Bowen, p. 20.

Cain, mark of. Burnam (1975), p. 42.

Calvary. McKenzie, p. 319.

Candles. McKenzie, p. 118.

Chapter and verse. Robinson, p. 161.

Cherubs. Hastings, p. 133.

Christ as a name. Burnam (1975), p. 49.

Christian. Hastings, p. 138.

Christmas. Burnam (1975), pp. 49–50.

Circle of the earth. *New Oxford Annotated*, p. 778.

"Cleanliness is next to godliness." Burnam (1975), p. 53.

Coat of many colors. *New Oxford Annotated*, p. 47; Bowen, p. 43–44.

Compass navigation. *Wycliffe*, p. 1176.

Creation. Finegan, p. 297.

Deaconness. Mickelsen, p. 26.

Demons vs. disease. *Harper*, p. 971.

Donkey in triumphal entry. McKenzie, p. 592.

Double share of Elisha. *Eerdman's Handbook*, p. 272.

Dove's dung. Smith, p. 148.

Eating and drinking. Gundry, p. 188.

Ecclesiastes. *Harper*, p. 971.

Eden, expulsion from. Burnam (1980), pp. 62–63; Gaster, pp. 48–49.

Eye for an eye. *Harper*, p. 113; *New Oxford Annotated*, p. 94.

Eye of a needle. Minear, p. 158; Miller, p. 482.

Firmament. Archer, p. 61; *New Oxford Annotated*, pp. 1, 9.

Fish as a Christian symbol. Burnam (1975), p. 94.

Frankincense. Hastings, p. 307.

Gad and Meni. Gaster, pp. 196–97; Smith, p. 396.

Gild the lily. Burnam (1975), p. 292.

"God tempers the wind to the shorn lamb." Burnam (1975), p. 107.

Gospel writers as disciples. Gundry, p. 102–3.

Groves. Miller, p. 238.

Hebrews, Israelites. *New Oxford Annotated*, pp. 336, 349; Miller, p. 250.

Hebrews, author of. *Abingdon*, p. 1297.

Helpmeet. Burnam (1975), p. 121.

"He may run that readeth." Holt, p. 299.

Hilarious givers. Carson, p. 33.

Hosanna. *New Oxford Annotated*, p. 768.

Household gods. Keller, p. 55.

"How knoweth this man letters?" Gundry, p. 160.

Inn. McKenzie, p. 389.

"In the beginning was the Word." Burnam (1975), p. 136.

"It is more blessed to give than to receive." Burnam (1975), p. 138.

"I will lift up mine eyes unto the hills." *New Oxford Annotated*, p. 754; Keel, p. 20.

Jacob's ladder. *Eerdman's Handbook*, p. 144; Miller, p. 377.

Jehovah. Hastings, p. 300.

Kingdom Come. Gundry, p. 144.

Kingdom of God vs. kingdom of heaven. Gundry, pp. 87, 144.

Last Supper. Gundry, p. 193.

Lazarus as a leper. Hastings, p. 538.

Leprosy. Hastings, pp. 575–76.

"Let us make man in our own image." *Wycliffe*, p. 4; *Harper*, p. 5.

Locusts as food. McKenzie, p. 516; Miller, pp. 274, 397.

Lucifer. Burnam (1975), p. 165.

Mammon. Hastings, pp. 95, 614.

Man in God's image. McKenzie, p. 12; Smith, p. 14.

Mary Magdalene as a prostitute. *Harper*, p. 1545.

Mary of Bethany as a woman of sin. *Harper*, p. 1545.

Meat and drink. Burnam (1980), p. 131.

Mess of pottage. Burnam (1980), p. 173.

Miracles. Grun, pp. 4–26; *Harper*, p. 1641.

Myrrh. Hastings, p. 682.

Offerings of Cain and Abel. Hastings, p. 2.

Onanism. Burnam (1975), p. 191.

Peace offerings. *Abingdon*, p. 280; *Almanac*, p. 403.

Peter as the gatekeeper of heaven. Hastings, pp. 742–43; Gundry, pp. 154–55.

Peter's cursing. *Wycliffe*, p. 1022.

Plucking corn. Gundry, p. 137.

"Pride goeth before a fall." Burnam (1975), p. 221.

Rahab the harlot. *Harper,* p. 316.

Red Sea, parting of. *New Oxford Annotated,* p. 84; *Harper,* p. 102.

Render unto Caesar. Gundry, pp. 184–85.

Revelations. Burnam (1975), p. 237.

Rose of Sharon. Hastings, p. 864.

Sabbath vs. Sunday. Hastings, pp. 866–67.

Sailing and the sea. *New Oxford Annotated,* p. 2.

Salome. Smith, p. 233.

Samson and Delilah. Burnam (1975), p. 245.

Samson, source of strength. *New Oxford Annotated,* p. 169.

Saul becoming Paul. Gundry, p. 224.

Scapegoat. Burnam (1975), p. 246.

Sermon on the Mount. Burnam (1975), p. 138; Gundry, p. 86.

Seventy times seven. Gundry, pp. 157–58.

"Spare the rod and spoil the child." Burnam (1975), p. 267.

Swords into ploughshares. Burnam (1975), p. 288.

Taking the Lord's name in vain. *New Oxford Annotated,* p. 93.

Three kings. Burnam (1975), pp. 288–89.

"Through a glass darkly." Miller, p. 449.

"Vengeance is mine saith the Lord." Burnam (1975), pp. 303–04.

Vinegar given to Jesus. *Jerusalem,* p. 43; *Harper,* p. 1525.

Vision of the dry bones. *New Oxford Annotated,* p. 1048.

Vocation as a "calling." Von Allmen, pp. 46–47.

"Where two or three are gathered." Gundry, p. 86.

Wisdom of Solomon. McKenzie, pp. 828–30.

Xmas. Burnam (1975), p. 329.

"Your zeal hath provoked many." Hastings, p. 769.

"You say that I am." *Wycliffe,* p. 1066.

Bibliography

The Abingdon Bible Commentary. Ed. by Frederick Carl Eiselen, et al. Nashville: Abingdon, 1929.

Archer, Gleason L. *Encyclopedia of Bible Difficulties.* Grand Rapids: Zondervan, 1982.

Bowen, Barbara M. *Strange Scriptures That Perplex the Western Mind.* Grand Rapids: Eerdmans, 1945.

Bright, John. *A History of Israel.* Philadelphia: Westminster, 1952.

Burnham, Tom. *The Dictionary of Misinformation.* New York: Ballantine, 1975.

_____. *More Misinformation.* New York: Ballantine, 1980.

Cornfeld, Gaalyahu, ed. *Pictorial Biblical Encyclopedia.* Tel Aviv: Hamikra Baolam, 1964.

Eerdman's Handbook to the Bible. Ed. by David Alexander and Pat Alexander. Grand Rapids: Eerdmans, 1973.

Finegan, Jack. *Handbook of Biblical Chronology.* Princeton: Princeton University, 1964.

Gaster, Theodore H. *Myth, Legend, and Custom in the Old Testament.* New York: Harper and Row, 1969.

Gundry, Robert H. *A Survey of the New Testament.* Grand Rapids, Mi.: Eerdmans, 1970.

Grun, Bernard. *The Timetables of History.* New York: Simon and Schuster, 1979.

Hastings, James. *Dictionary of the Bible.* Rev. ed. by Frederick C. Grant and H. H. Rowley. New York: Charles Scribner's, 1963.

Harper Study Bible. Ed. by Harold Lindsell. New York: Harper and Row, 1964.

Holt, John Marshall. "So He May Run Who Reads It." *Journal of Biblical Literature,* 83(1964), 298–302.

The Jerusalem Bible. Garden City, N.Y.: Doubleday, 1968.

Keel, Othmar. *The Symbolism of the Biblical World.* Trans. by Timothy J. Hallett. New York: Seabury, 1978.

Keller, Werner. *The Bible as History in Pictures.* New York: William Morrow, 1963.

McKenzie, John L. *Dictionary of the Bible.* New York: Macmillan, 1979.

Mickelson, Berkeley and Alvera. "Does Male Dominance Tarnish Our Translations?" *Christianity Today,* October 5, 1979, pp. 23–29.

Miller, Madeleine S., and J. Lane Miller. *The New Harper's Bible Dictionary.* New York: Harper and Row, 1973.

Minear, Paul. "Eye of the Needle." *Journal of Biblical Literature,* 16(1942), 157–69.

The New Oxford Annotated Bible with the Apocrypha. Ed. by Herbert G. May and Bruce M. Metzger. New York: Oxford University, 1973.

The Bible Almanac. Ed. by James I. Packer, et al. Nashville: Thomas Nelson, 1980.

Rachleff, Owen S. *Exploring the Bible.* New York: Abbeville Press, 1981.

Robinson, Gordon. *New Testament Detection.* New York: Oxford University, 1964.

Smith, William. *Smith's Bible Dictionary.* New York: Berkeley, 1985.

Strong, James. *The New Strong's Exhaustive Concordance of the Bible.* Nashville: Thomas Nelson, 1984.

A Companion to the Bible. Ed. by J.–J. Von Allmen. New York: Oxford University, 1958.

The Wycliffe Bible Commentary. Ed. by Charles F. Pfeiffer and Everett F. Harrison. Chicago: Moody, 1972.

Index of Scripture References

Index of Scripture References

215